Doggin' Asheville

The 50 Best Places
To Hike With Your Dog
In The Carolina Blue Ridge

DOUG GELBERT

illustrations by

ANDREW CHESWORTH

CRUDEN BAY BOOKS

There is always a new trail to look forward to...

DOGGIN' ASHEVILLE: THE 50 BEST PLACES TO HIKE
WITH YOUR DOG IN THE CAROLINA BLUE RIDGE

Cruden Bay Books
PO Box 467
Montchanin, DE 19710
www.hikewithyourdog.com

International Standard Book Number 978-1-935771-22-7

"Dogs are our link to paradise...to sit with a dog on a hillside
on a glorious afternoon is to be back in Eden,
where doing nothing was not boring - it was peace."
- Milan Kundera

Ahead On The Trail

Introduction

Asheville can be a great place to hike with your dog. Within a short drive your canine adventurer can be climbing mountains that leave him panting, trotting through impossibly green ravines, or exploring some of America's most spectacular waterfalls or hiking.

Sometimes the best canine hike comes by parking beside an old forest jeep road and disappearing with your dog for hours of solitude in the woods. I have sought out more formal day-hiking fare and selected what I consider to be the 50 best places to take your dog for an outing around Asheville and ranked them according to subjective criteria including the variety of hikes available, opportunities for canine swimming and pleasure of the walks. The rankings include a mix of parks that feature long walks and parks that contain short walks. Did I miss your favorite? Let us know at *hikewithyourdog.com*.

For dog owners it is important to realize that not all parks are open to our best trail companions (see page 14 for a list of parks that do not allow dogs). It is sometimes hard to believe but not everyone loves dogs. We are, in fact, in the minority when compared with our non-dog owning neighbors.

So when visiting a park always keep your dog under control and clean up any messes and we can all expect our great parks to remain open to our dogs. And maybe some others will see the light as well. *Remember, every time you go out with your dog you are an ambassador for all dog owners.*

Grab that leash and hit the trail!
DBG

Hiking With Your Dog

So you want to start hiking with your dog. Hiking with your dog can be a fascinating way to explore the Asheville region from a canine perspective. Some things to consider:

🐾 Dog's Health

Hiking can be a wonderful preventative for any number of physical and behavioral disorders. One in every three dogs is overweight and running up trails and leaping through streams is great exercise to help keep pounds off. Hiking can also relieve boredom in a dog's routine and calm dogs prone to destructive habits. And hiking with your dog strengthens the overall owner/dog bond.

🐾 Breed of Dog

All dogs enjoy the new scents and sights of a trail. But some dogs are better suited to hiking than others. If you don't as yet have a hiking companion, select a breed that matches your interests. Do you look forward to an entire afternoon's hiking? You'll need a dog bred to keep up with such a pace, such as a retriever or a spaniel. Is a half-hour enough walking for you? It may not be for an energetic dog like a border collie. If you already have a hiking friend, tailor your plans to his abilities.

🐾 Conditioning

Just like humans, dogs need to be acclimated to the task at hand. An inactive dog cannot be expected to bounce from the easy chair in the den to complete a 3-hour hike. You must also be physically able to restrain your dog if confronted with distractions on the trail (like a scampering squirrel or a pack of joggers). Have your dog checked by a veterinarian before significantly increasing his activity level.

🐾 Weather

Hot humid summers do not do dogs any favors. With no sweat glands and only panting available to disperse body heat, dogs are much more susceptible to heat stroke than we are. Unusually rapid panting and/or a bright red tongue are signs of heat exhaustion in your pet.

Always carry enough water for your hike. Even the prime hiking days of late fall through early spring that don't seem too warm can cause discomfort in dark-coated dogs if the sun is shining brightly. During cold snaps, short-coated breeds may require additional attention.

☙ Trail Hazards

Dogs won't get poison ivy but they can transfer it to you. Some trails are littered with small pieces of broken glass that can slice a dog's paws. Nasty thorns can also blanket trails that we in shoes may never notice.

☙ Ticks

You won't be able to spend much time in North Carolina woods without encountering ticks. All are nasty but the deer tick - no bigger than a pin head - carries with it the spectre of Lyme disease. Lyme disease attacks a dog's joints and makes walking painful. The tick needs to be embedded in the skin to transmit Lyme disease. It takes 4-6 hours for a tick to become embedded and another 24-48 hours to transmit Lyme disease bacteria.

When hiking, walk in the middle of trails away from tall grass and bushes. And when the summer sun fades away don't stop thinking about ticks - they remain active any time the temperature is above 30 degrees. By checking your dog - and yourself - thoroughly after each walk you can help avoid Lyme disease. Ticks tend to congregate on your dog's ears, between the toes and around the neck and head.

☙ Water

Surface water, including fast-flowing streams, is likely to be infested with a microscopic protozoa called *Giardia*, waiting to wreak havoc on a dog's intestinal system. The most common symptom is crippling diarrhea. Algae, pollutants and contaminants can all be in streams, ponds and puddles. If possible, carry fresh water for your dog on the trail - your dog can even learn to drink happily from a squirt bottle.

·ᶻᵃ· Rattlesnakes and Copperheads, etc.

Rattlesnakes and their close cousins, copperheads, are not particularly aggressive animals but you should treat any venomous snake with respect and keep your distance. A rattler's colors may vary but they are recognized by the namesake rattle on the tail and a diamond-shaped head. Unless cornered or teased by humans or dogs, a rattlesnake will crawl away and avoid striking. Avoid placing your hand in unexamined rocky areas and crevasses and try and keep your dog from putting his nose in such places as well. Stick to the trail and out of high grass where you can't see well. If you hear a nearby rattle, stop immediately and hold your dog back. Identify where the snake is and slowly back away.

If you or your dog is bitten, do not panic but get to a hospital or veterinarian with as little physical movement as possible. Wrap between the bite and the heart. Rattlesnakes might give "dry bites" where no poison is injected, but you should always check with a doctor after a bite even if you feel fine.

·ᶻᵃ· Porcupines

Porcupines are easy for a curious dog to catch and that makes them among the most dangerous animals you may meet because an embedded quill is not only painful but can cause infection if not properly removed.

🐾 Black Bears

Are you likely to see a bear while out hiking with your dog? No, it's not likely. It is, however, quite a thrill if you are fortunate enough to spot a black bear on the trail - from a distance.

Black bear attacks are incredibly rare. In the year 2000 a hiker was killed by a black bear in Great Smoky National Park and it was the first deadly bear attack in the 66-year history of America's most popular national park. It was the first EVER in the southeastern United States. In all of North America only 43 black bear mauling deaths have ever been recorded (through 1999).

Most problems with black bears occur near a campground (like the above incident) where bears have learned to forage for unprotected food. On the trail bears will typically see you and leave the area. What should you do if you encounter a black bear? Experts agree on three important things:

1) Never run. A bear will outrun you, outclimb you, outswim you. Don't look like prey.
2) Never get between a female bear and a cub who may be nearby feeding.
3) Leave a bear an escape route.

If the bear is at least 15 feet away and notices you make sure you keep your dog close and calm. If a bear stands on its hind legs or comes closer it may just be trying to get a better view or smell to evaluate the situation. Wave your arms and make noise to scare the bear away. Most bears will quickly leave the area.

If you encounter a black bear at close range, stand upright and make yourself appear as large a foe as possible. Avoid direct eye contact and speak in a calm, assertive and assuring voice as you back up slowly and out of danger.

Outfitting Your Dog For A Hike

These are the basics for taking your dog on a hike:

▸ **Collar.**
 A properly fitting collar should not be so loose as to come off but you should be able to slide your flat hand under the collar.

▸ **Identification Tags.**
 Get one with your veterinarian's phone number as well.

▸ **Bandanna.**
 Can help distinguish him from game in hunting season.

▸ **Leash.**
 Leather lasts forever but if there's water in your dog's future, consider quick-drying nylon.

▸ **Water.**
 Carry 8 ounces for every hour of hiking.

🐾 *I want my dog to help carry water, snacks and other supplies on the trail. Where do I start?*
To select an appropriate dog pack measure your dog's girth around the rib cage. A dog pack should fit securely without hindering the dog's ability to walk normally.

🐾 *Will my dog wear a pack?*
Wearing a dog pack is no more obtrusive than wearing a collar, although some dogs will take to a pack easier than others. Introduce the pack by draping a towel over your dog's back in the house and then having your dog wear an empty pack on short walks. Progressively add some crumpled newspaper and then bits of clothing. Fill the pack with treats and reward your dog from the stash. Soon your dog will associate the dog pack with an outdoor adventure and will eagerly look forward to wearing it.

❧ *How much weight can I put into a dog pack?*

Many dog packs are sold by weight recommendations. A healthy, well-conditioned dog can comfortably carry 25% to 33% of its body weight. Breeds prone to back problems or hip dysplasia should not wear dog packs. Consult your veterinarian before stuffing the pouches with gear.

❧ *How does a dog wear a pack?*

The pack, typically with cargo pouches on either side, should ride as close to the shoulders as possible without limiting movement. The straps that hold the dog pack in place should be situated where they will not cause chafing.

❧ *What are good things to put in a dog pack?*

Low density items such as food and poop bags are good choices. Ice cold bottles of water can cool your dog down on hot days. Don't put anything in a dog pack that can break. Dogs will bang the pack on rocks and trees as they wiggle through tight spots in the trail. Dogs also like to lie down in creeks and other wet spots so seal items in plastic bags. A good use for dog packs when on day hikes around the Carolina Blue Ridge is trail maintenance - your dog can pack out trash left by inconsiderate visitors before you.

🐾 *Are dog booties a good idea?*

Although not typically necessary, dog booties can be an asset, especially for the occasional canine hiker whose paw pads have not become toughened. Trails can be rocky and in some places there may be broken glass or roots. Hiking boots for dogs are designed to prevent pads from cracking while trotting across rough surfaces.

🐾 *What should a doggie first aid kit include?*

Even when taking short hikes it is a good idea to have some basics available for emergencies:

- ▶ 4" square gauze pads
- ▶ cling type bandaging tapes
- ▶ topical wound disinfectant cream
- ▶ tweezers
- ▶ insect repellent - no reason to leave your dog unprotected against mosquitoes and biting flies
- ▶ veterinarian's phone number

The Other End Of The Leash

Leash laws are like speed limits - everyone seems to have a private interpretation of their validity. Some dog owners never go outside with an unleashed dog; others treat the laws as suggestions or disregard them completely. It is not the purpose of this book to tell dog owners where to go to evade the leash laws or reveal the parks where rangers will look the other way at an unleashed dog. Nor is it the business of this book to preach vigilant adherence to the leash laws. Nothing written in a book is going to change people's behavior with regard to leash laws. So this will be the last time leash laws are mentioned, save occasionally when we point out the parks where dogs are welcomed off leash.

Low Impact Hiking
With Your Dog

Every time you hike with your dog on the trail you are an ambassador for all dog owners. Some people you meet won't believe in your right to take a dog on the trail. Be friendly to all and make the best impression you can by practicing low impact hiking with your dog:

- Pack out everything you pack in.

- Do not leave dog scat on the trail; if you haven't brought plastic bags for poop removal bury it away from the trail and topical water sources.

- Hike only where dogs are allowed.

- Stay on the trail.

- Do not allow your dog to chase wildlife.

- Step off the trail and wait with your dog while horses and other hikers pass.

- Do not allow your dog to bark - people are enjoying the trail for serenity.

- *Have as much fun on your hike as your dog does.*

The Best of the Best

- **BEST CANINE HIKE TO A VIEW**
  Max Patch

- **BEST HIKE TO MEET OTHER DOGS**
  Richmond Hill Park

- **BEST HIKE TO NOT SEE ANOTHER DOG**
  Green River Trails

- **BEST 1-HOUR WORKOUT FOR YOUR DOG**
  Holmes Education State Forest - Demonstration Trail

- **BEST CANINE HIKE TO A WATERFALL**
  Cove Creek Falls

- **BEST CANINE SWIMMING HOLE - RIVER**
  Warren Wilson College Trails - River Trail

- **BEST CANINE SWIMMING HOLE - LAKE**
  Fawn Lake - DuPont State Forest

- **BEST PLACE TO HIKE ALL DAY WITH YOUR DOG**
  Pisgah National Forest - Shining Rock Wilderness

- **PRETTIEST HIKE WITH YOUR DOG**
  North Carolina Arboretum

- **BEST HIKE TO RUINS WITH YOUR DOG**
  Rattlesnake Lodge

No Dogs

Before we get started on the best places to take your dog, let's get out of the way some of the parks that do not allow dogs at all:

Botanical Gardens of Asheville - Asheville
Pearson's Falls - Saluda
Riverview Cemetery - Asheville
Rough Creek Watershed - Canton
Western North Carolina Nature Center - Asheville

O.K. that wasn't too bad. Let's forget about these and move on to some of the great places where we CAN take our dogs on Asheville area trails...

The 50 Best Places To Hike With Your Dog Around Asheville...

1
Black Balsam Knob Trailhead

The Park

Balds are found primarily in the Southern Appalachians, where the climate is too warm to support an alpine zone—upper areas where trees fail to grow due to short or non-existent growing seasons—even at the highest elevations. Why some summits are bald and some are not is a mystery to scientists. There are two types of balds - heath balds with blankets of evergreen shrubs and grassy balds covered with dense swards of native grasses. Black Balsam Knob is a grassy bald and at 6,214 feet, the highest in the Blue Ridge.

Transylvania County

Phone Number
- (828) 257-4200

Website
- fs.usda.gov/main/nfsnc

Admission Fee
- None

Park Hours
- Sunrise to sundown although Parkway access closes in winter

Directions
- *Blue Ridge Parkway*, Milepost 420. Black Balsam is not a Parkway attraction but a part of Pisgah National Forest so it is not signed; turn onto FS 816 (paved).

The Walks

How good is the canine hiking here? There are some who will tell you the three miles of unobstructed views across Black Balsam Knob and neighboring Tennant Mountain comprise the best hike they have ever taken with their dog. And that may not even be the best hike at Black Balsam.

The quickest way to the summit is on the *Art Loeb Trail* from where it crosses the access road (no trailhead signage but the line of cars will define it). After a scenic ten-minute climb in the thick balsam firs you are in the wide open expanses with views of the Blue Ridge Mountains in every direction for the next hour. You can close your loop with the *Investor Gap Trail*; backpackers can continue on to Cold Mountain of literary and Hollywood fame that you admire in the distance to the north.

Matching canine hiking on Black Balsam Knob stride for stride in "wow" moments is the moderate climb to the Sam Knob summit on the opposite side of the trailhead lot. Combine the journey with the *Flat Laurel Creek Trail* for a superlative loop with your dog across meadows, stands of wild blueberries and your standard rhododendron and rock outcrops. Sam Knob is another bald, albeit with clumps of shrubs so you will shift around the mountaintop to allow your dog to soak in the 360-degree views.

What must dogs think when they reach views like the ones on Black Balsam Knob?

Trail Sense: This is a wilderness area with sparse markings at best; maps can be found online.

Dog Friendliness
Dogs can hike on this National Forest land.
Traffic
Foot traffic only; summers are busy here almost every day.
Canine Swimming
Flat Laurel Creek will provide little more than a splash for your dog.
Trail Time
Your dog can tag the summit of Black Balsam Knob and return in an hour but most canine hikers will spend much more time than that here.

2
DuPont
State Forest

The Park

The E.I. du Pont de Nemours Company began on a pristine stream in northern Delaware in 1802 to grind explosive black powder. In the 1950s, by then an international chemical giant, the DuPont Company once again went searching for pure water and crisp air but this time it was to manufacture sensitive X-ray film. They landed in 12,000-acre Buck Forest outside Brevard where the DuPont plant was the first in the country to conjure up medical X-ray films on polyester film. In 1996 DuPont sold its facility to Sterling Diagnostic Imaging of Houston and 2,700 acres surrounding the plant. The remaining land was sold to the State for conservation for nickels on the dollar and this became the foundation for the 10,415-acre DuPont State Forest. The diva of the forest is the Little River that makes several picturesque plunges, each unique in its own way, as it flows through the property making the forest the star of Transylvania County's "Land of Waterfalls."

Henderson/Transylvania counties

Phone Number
- (828) 877-6527

Website
- dupontforest.com

Admission Fee
- None

Park Hours
- Sunrise to sunset

Directions
- *Cedar Mountain*; between Brevard and Hendersonville. From US 64 take Crab Creek Road east to Staton Road, turning at the brown forest sign. Continue up the mountain to parking areas described below.

Your dog can explore Bridal Veil Falls from the top and the bottom.

The Walks

There are more than 90 - yes, 90 - named trails in DuPont State Forest, all of which are open to your dog. Let's take a look at what's in store for your best trail companion at each of the six parking access areas in the forest:

Hooker Falls. This is where most waterfall hunters will land and it is the most crowded and least inviting for dog owners. If you have never seen Hooker Falls or Triple Falls or High Falls you will have to vault the metal guardrail with your dog and walk up *Triple Falls Trail* - a short, but steep one mile - at least once.

A trail/stairs will lead to the middle of Triple Falls.

Lake Imaging. The lot on the left at the bottom of the hill before Hooker Falls, this is a favorite launching point for equestrians. A superb canine hiking loop can be crafted here with the *Ridgeline Trail* and the *Jim Branch Trail*, one of the prettiest footpaths in the entire forest. Unusual for DuPont Forest, water plays almost no role in the canine hiking in this section of the park, save for the namesake pond that offers a refreshing doggie dip at the end of an adventure.

High Falls. Another popular lot for casual hikers hunting waterfalls. The trotting here is mostly on service roads that probe the interior of the forest - and you can chance to see the occasional vehicle on these roads. Once you pass through the covered bridge big walks await your dog, including to Wintergreen Falls, the most remote hydro-spectactacular in the forest where the stream

Your dog may have seen High Falls in the movie *The Last of the Mohicans*.

19

makes a hard left turn. Your dog's best hiking here will be on the *Lake Dense Trail* that is foot traffic only and leads to a pretty woodland pond with a dock for diving dogs.

The dog paddling is easy in Lake Dense.

Guion Farm. This lot off Sky Valley Road is a good place to create hiking loops of a half-hour or more through an attractive mixed forest including on the *Shoal Creek Trail* and *Hickory Mountain Road*, which features some open-air hiking around the farm. This is also a place to tag Stone Mountain, the highest point in the forest at 3,620 feet, although the peak has its own small parking area 1.5 miles further up Sky Valley Road at the Rocky Ridge Trailhead. From Guion Farm the elevation gain is over 1,000 feet but the hard pulling doesn't begin until the narrow *Stone Mountain Trail* is reached. Don't let the tame ridgeline lull your dog into thinking the climb is over before the final ascent to the summit. Your purchase on these slabs of granite are views across the entire DuPont State Forest.

Corn Mill Shoals. This parking area on Cascade Lake Road is a popular one for mountain bikers, with several destinations awaiting. A rocky passage leads up to a slickrock crossing of Cedar Rock and the loop closes from the top of Bridal Veils Falls, where the Little River begins its long slide down the granite face, to a wooded jaunt along the river itself. The shoals are reached from a wide trail of their own but savvy canine hikers will want to detour off the *Corn Mill Shoals Trail* for the *Burnt Mountain Trail*, one of the best loops to take with your dog in DuPont forest. On the parking lot side of Cascade Lake Road, guide your dog across the one-step stream to the south and pick up the *Wilkie Trail* that leads to a seldom-used loop that crosses an open rock face and works back up a farm road and down an abandoned quarry. All good dog hiking stuff.

Fawn Lake. The park's most remote lot on Reasonover Road also offers up some of the most solitary canine hiking in the forest down the *Reasonover Creek Trail*. It can also be the shortest if you come after a hard rain and the wet-paw crossing of the creek is impassable. In the opposite direction is Fawn Lake and it may be impossible to get your water-loving dog to hike past this enchanting canine swimming hole. Beyond the lake, however, is some excellent open-air trotting along the *Airstrip Trail*.

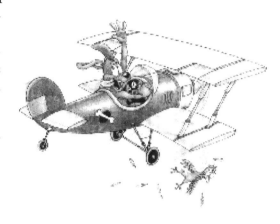

Trail Sense: Superlative color trail maps are available from area tourist centers - but not on site. The trails are marked at the many junctions but you will really need the map before your come. The map also grades the difficulty of the trails to help you match your canine hiking day in DuPont State Forest to your dog's abilities.

Dog Friendliness
Dogs are allowed to hike all the trails in DuPont State Forest.

Traffic
This is a popular spot with mountain bikers and nearly all of the forest away from the Little River waterfalls is open to hunting so take heed of the seasonal hunting dates.

Canine Swimming
The lakes in the forest make worthy destinations for your trail dog but the streams are only deep enough for splashing and cooling off most of the year.

Trail Time
You can find hikes for your dog of less than one hour to a full day and more in DuPont State Forest.

3
Montreat Trails

The Park

The Reverend John C. Collins led a congregation of clergy and lay leaders into the North Carolina mountains in 1897 and purchased 4,500 pristine high-mountain acres for a Christian settlement called Montreat, a mashing of "mountain retreat." A lodge was accepting its first guests by 1901. A Presbyterian church and a women's college preparatory school - first class of eight students - soon followed. It 1934 the institution was renamed Montreat College and today it operates as a four-year college with several campuses.

In 1911 the Mount Mitchell Railroad ran across the Presbyterian grounds at Montreat on its 21-mile journey from a junction with the Southern Railway in the town of Black Mountain to Camp Alice, just one-half mile from the summit of Mount Mitchell. The quarry was spruce pine and when it was all chopped down the owners converted the railroad bed into the "Mount Mitchell Motor Road," a cinder-surfaced, one-way toll road to the top of the highest peak in the eastern United States. Tourism was so popular that a second toll road was built up the east flank of the Black Mountains and these old trackways help form much of the Montreat Trails.

Buncombe County
Phone Number
- (800) 572-2257
Website
- montreat.org
Admission Fee
- None
Park Hours
- Sunrise to sunset
Directions
- *Black Mountain*; from I-40 take Exit 64 onto Route 9 through town and through the Montreat gate. When Assembly Drive bears right stay straight to the Graybeard Trail.

The Walks

There are enough peaks and canine hikes at Montreat that you could take you dog out every day for a week and not set a paw on the same stretch of trail. Sooner or later every canine adventure who frequents these trails, however, will make the climb to Graybeard Mountain, the highest elevation on the property at 5,408 feet. The quickest way is on the 4.75-mile *Graybeard Trail* that can roughly be divided into the three 45-minute to an hour chunks. The first leg climbs steadily up Flat Creek with three normally easy stream crossings and numerous chances for your dog to step off the trail into an enticing pool under a small waterfall. Expect as many pawfalls on rock as on dirt during this opening thrust. Once at Pot Cove Gap the trail boards the Old Trestle Road for almost flat trotting on to Graybeard Falls, a sheet of water flowing down a rockface - and more splashing. The final push for the summit with its west- and east-facing views reverts to a steady footpath climb. Take a five-minute detour at the trail shelter just past the falls to scramble up to the craggy overlook at Walker's Knob where the entire Montreat Valley will spread beneath your dog's paws.

Not every canine hike at Montreat need be a plunge into the 2,500-acre wilderness with options such as the mile-long interpretive *Gate Trail* at the Nature Center, the *Horseshoe Loop* on nearby Lookout Road and a 1.7-mile sampler loop of the *Graybeard Trail-Harry Bryan Trail-Julia Woodward Trail-Sanctuary Trail.*

Trail Sense: With 20+ miles of trails you will need a map which can be pulled off the website or a detailed one purchased in the Nature Center.

Dog Friendliness
Dogs are welcome on the Montreat Trails.

Traffic
Bikes and four-wheelers are confined to the *Old Mitchell Toll Road* and a couple of others.

Canine Swimming
The Old Reservoir at the Graybeard Trailhead makes a splendid place for your dog to cool off and practice her dogpaddle strokes after a signature long Montreat hike.

Trail Time
Many, many hours possible.

4
Pisgah Center for Wildlife Education

The Park

The distillery-clear waters of the Davidson River make every list of America's top trout streams and is the centerpiece for the Pisgah Center for Wildlife Education along its banks. Dedicated to educating and exploring North Carolina wildlife, its free classes on outdoor skills, photography and fly-fishing fill up months in advance. For canine hikers there are two destinations here - the closer and more popular John Rock and the more distant Cedar Rock Mountain.

Transylvania County

Phone Number
- (828) 877-4423

Website
- ncwildlife.org/Learning/EducationCenters/Pisgah

Admission Fee
- None

Park Hours
- Sunrise to sunset

Directions
- *Pisgah National Forest*; from the Visitor Center on US 276 go 3.5 miles north and turn left on FS 475. Go 1.5 miles to the Center.

The Walks

You can see John Rock looming over the parking lot so you know where you are headed and it is a circuitous route indeed. The *John Rock Trail* is a loop at the back of the *Cat Gap Loop*, which is best done counterclockwise to save the refreshing waters of Davidson River for your dog until the end. Part of the trail utilizes old railroad grades which extract some, just some, of the sting from the ascent. Once on top your dog will be face-to-face with Looking Glass Rock - back from the edge of course.

Cedar Rock Mountain is a conical-shaped pluton that rises over 4,000 feet - higher than its more celebrated neighbors to its north. The *Butter Gap Trail*, which travels though open areas of Pickelsimer Fields before setting your dog to panting with a straight up climb, and the *Art Loeb Trail* form a loop off the *Cat Gap Loop* to access its south and east-facing views from Sandy Gap. Unmaintained trails around Cedar Rock will enable you to scramble carefully with your dog to more vantage points.

While the views get top billing here it is the uncredited waterfalls that will delight your dog more. Coming up the western side of *Cat Gap Loop* keep an eye out for a narrow dirt path that drops away to a hidden falls on Cedar Rock Creek. Just upstream at a campsite is another cascade with good dog paddling in the plunge pool. Falls on Grogan Creek can be ferreted out on the left side of *Butter Gap Trail*, about fifteen minutes past the junction with the *Long Branch Trail*.

Your dog will need to go off trail to find this waterfall.

Trail Sense: The trails begins behind a gated road next to the Wildlife Center. The key junctions are signed but there are enough multi-trail intersections and service roads to make you want to keep a map handy.

Dog Friendliness
Dogs are allowed to hike on these trails.
Traffic
Seasonal mountain bike use but mostly foot traffic.
Canine Swimming
The Cat Gap Loop finishes along almost a mile of Davidson River frontage. If fishermen aren't pursuing the brown trout that favors deep pools, this is the perfect cool down to a long trail day for your dog.
Trail Time
You can make it up to John Rock and back in less than two hours but typically block out a full day of canine hiking here.

5
Harmon Den Area

The Park

Harmon's "den" was, according to local lore, a rocky outcropping a woodsman named Harmon called home. Although today Interstate 40 is practically the only paved road through this remote region a century ago these mountains were laced with logging roads and narrow gauge railroads. Timber companies cut and carted out just about every tree in the Cold Springs Creek watershed. The stripped hillsides were an easy buy for the Forest Service in 1936. Today the unrivaled star of Harmon Den Area is Max Patch Mountain, named after the farmer who cleared the mountain in the 1800s for cattle grazing which continued until 1982 when the U.S. Department of Agriculture parried a developer's plan to build a ski resort and bought 392 acres atop the 4,629-foot summit. Max Patch is the southernmost bald on the *Appalachian Trail* and often referred to as one of its "crown jewels." But it is not a natural bald - the Forest Service keeps the peak grassy with tractors.

Haywood County

Phone Number
- (828) 682-6146

Website
- fs.usda.gov/main/nfsnc

Admission Fee
- None

Park Hours
- Sunrise to sunset

Directions
- *Pisgah National Forest*; easiest of several way in is to take I-40 to Exit 7 onto Cold Springs Creek Road (gravel). Follow the road 6 miles to its end at Max Patch Road (not signed). Turn left and travel up 1.5 miles to parking area on the right.

The Walks

From the often too-small parking lot, your dog can be on the summit of Max Patch before she shakes the dust out of her ears from the journey up the mountain on one of the several gravel approach roads. A grassy path and easy five-minute walk lead straight to the bare mountaintop. But most canine hikers will angle left and set off on the loop trails that send your dog through a light forest before depositing him on the grassy expanses. At the junction with the *Appalachian Trail* the short loop goes hard right to cross the summit lawn less than 200 yards away before dropping down the mountain and finishing the loop. The 2.4-mile longer loop around the mountain dips into the countryside below and bears left - it won't actually cross the summit but your dog won't let you forget to tag the top of Max Patch with its easily purchased, unparalleled views. On display are the Black Mountains to the northeast, the Newfound Mountains across the parking lot and the Great Smoky Mountains across Tennessee to the west, if you need to put some names to the endless protrusions surrounding you.

You can extend your dog's hiking day below the Max Patch summit by joining the *Buckeye Ridge* horse trail (marked only if traveling in a counterclockwise direction) or along the *Appalachian Trail* in either direction. If your dog has wearied of the crowds you can duck down a less-traveled horse trail in Harmon Den where 50+ miles of mostly old logging roads trails dissect the backcountry.

There are views atop Max Patch Mountain in every direction.

Trail Sense: A mapboard, signs and the pawprints of others lead the way around Max Patch.

Dog Friendliness
Dogs are allowed to hike the *Appalachian Trail* and the forest roads.

Traffic
Foot traffic only on Max Patch.

Canine Swimming
Only seasonal trickles on Max Patch but if you have come via I-40 the Cold Springs Picnic Area on your way out offers an easy, refreshing cool-down spot.

Trail Time
One to two hours with many more possible.

6
Warren Wilson College Trails

The Park

Warren Wilson College began life in 1894 as the Asheville Farm School with 25 boys attending the first three grades of elementary instruction, guided by the Women's Board of Home Missions of the Presbyterian Church. Over the decades it evolved into a secondary school, acquiring the name of a church official, and emerged in 1972 as a four year-college. Today, in addition to their classwork, students are required to perform at least 100 hours of community service and work on-campus for the institution which operates a 300-acre working farm and maintains a 600-acre forest boasting 25 miles of hiking trails, most of which, save for the *Suicide Ridge Trails*, are open to the public.

Buncombe County

Phone Number
- (828) 298-3325

Website
- polarismaps.com/portfoli/wwc.pdf

Admission Fee
- None

Park Hours
- Sunrise to sunset

Directions
- *Swannanoa*; take Exit 55 off I-40 and pick up US 70 East. Turn left on Warren Wilson Road at the sign. For *Jones Mountain Trails* turn left on College View to the trailhead up the hill on the left. For the *River Trail* stay on Warren Wilson Road and park just across the Swannanoa River on the left. For *Dam Pasture Trails* turn left on Riceville Road and park across from Berea Church.

The Walks

The star walk on the college grounds is the *River Trail* which, if your dog loves to swim, will be the longest two-mile hike you ever take. The easy-going waters of the Swannanoa River are a perfect complement for the pace of your stroll along the flat dirt path. There are deep pools and riffles the entire way but the best doggie swimming hole comes at the beaches when the river starts a 180-degree turn. The trail doesn't leave the water until the last half-mile where it joins up with the *Dam Pasture Trail* and carries another mile to a parking area if you have a car shuttle. Otherwise it is back the way you came for more swimming and close up views of the Warren

Wilson farm where your dog can channel his inner cattle dog.

For a stiffer test for your dog there are the *Dam Pasture Trails* and the *Jones Mountain Trails*, both of which make ample use of old farm roads on exceedingly paw-friendly paths. There is only a brief visit to Bull Creek under the pines in Dam Pasture and no water at all on the climb to 2,753-foot Jones Mountain (winter views only

It doesn't get any better than the Swannanoa River for your water-loving dog.

at the summit) so your dog may demand a return trip to the *River Trail* before you leave campus.

Trail Sense: There are no maps or blazes on-site, only trailhead signs. The trail names on the online map at the listed website don't match the trails on the ground but you shouldn't get too confused with it in hand.

Dog Friendliness
Dogs are allowed to hike the trails, albeit behind the most soul-crushing "Leashed Dogs Only" signs in Asheville.
Traffic
Foot traffic only on the *River Trail*; bikes elsewhere and horses at Dam Pasture.
Canine Swimming
More swimming than hiking on the *River Trail*.
Trail Time
Your dog's day can stretch to a half-day and more at Warren Wilson College.

7
Pink Beds
Picnic Area

The Park

When George W. Vanderbilt purchased 125,000 acres for his Biltmore Estate much of the land was severely over-farmed and in drastic need of reforestation. Vanderbilt turned the task over to Gifford Pinchot, the first private forester hired in America. When his friend Theodore Roosevelt became President in 1900, Gifford Pinchot was named the first Chief Forester of the United States Forest Service. During his tenure, national forests would triple in size to 193 million acres. Back in Asheville, Vanderbilt hired Carl Schenck, a German versed in scientific forestry, to take command of the Biltmore forests. Schenck founded America's first school of forestry, the Biltmore Forest School, which graduated nearly 400 students with expertise and practical experience in forest management until it closed in 1913. The Cradle of Forestry National Historic Site in the Pink Beds was established by Congress in 1968 to preserve the legacy of the old Biltmore Forest School. The 6,500-acre Pink Beds takes it name, naturally enough, from the profusion of pink wildflowers that bloom in this flat, hemmed-in valley every spring.

Transylvania County

Phone Number
- (828) 877-3265

Website
- fs.usda.gov/nfsnc

Admission Fee
- None for Pink Beds; per person entrance fee for Cradle of Forestry but free on Tuesdays

Park Hours
- Sunrise to sunset at Pink Beds; 9:00 a.m. to 5:00 p.m. at Cradle of Forestry, mid-April until October

Directions
- *Pisgah National Forest*; take US 276 south from Milepost 412 of the Blue Ridge Parkway four miles to parking on the left (all paved).

The Walks

In the more than half-million acres of the Pisgah National Forest, the *Pink Beds Loop* is the easiest extended hiking you will find with your top trail companion. The loop winds lazily through mature oak-dominated hardwoods with a spattering of white pine stands in the cove forest but the dominant feature is the rare mountain bog. Sometimes the Pink Beds are too-well lubricated and impassable; even in dry times expect wet feet and paws. The *Pink Beds Loop* covers five miles but can be short-cutted across the wetlands on the *Bennett Branch Trail*.

Next door, the Cradle of Forestry sports two paved interpretive trails of about a mile in length - the *Forest Festival Trail* that focuses on forest products and includes an antique portable sawmill and a 1915 Climax locomotive. This 2-speed, geared steam engine was popular with loggers and more than a thousand were produced between 1888 and 1928. The *Biltmore Campus Trail* snakes through the rustic campus where many restored historic buildings still reside.

Trail Sense: The Pink Beds trails are well-signed.

Dog Friendliness
Dogs are allowed on the trails and in the picnic area.
Traffic
Primarily foot traffic; the Pink Beds are a popular group spot.
Canine Swimming
Some of the best doggie dips in the Blue Ridge await in the Bennett Branch.
Trail Time
At least two hours.

8
Carl Sandburg Home National Historic Site

The Park

In 1945 at the age of 67 Carl Sandburg, widely lauded as the "Poet of the People," had accomplished enough for two lifetimes. He left school at 13 to go to work and help his Swedish immigrant parents in Illinois. In his teens he traveled the country as a hobo and then fought briefly in the Spanish-American War. Afterwards he landed a job as a newspaper writer and established himself as a crusading investigative reporter and champion of labor rights. An inveterate collector of folk songs, Sandburg became a popular lecturer and in 1926 recorded an album of songs for the RCA Victor Talking Machine Company. Turning his talents to research he became known as the biographer of Abraham Lincoln and won a Pulitzer Prize for history in 1940 for four-volume set *Abraham Lincoln: The War Years*.

So when the Sandburgs packed up their belongings, including 16,000 books, onto a train in Michigan and moved to the Connemara Farm on the slopes of Glassy Mountain it could be expected he was ready to relax. Not so. After fixing up the 1839 Greek Revival house that had been built as a summer home for South Carolina political leader and first Secretary of the Treasury for the Confederate States of America, Christopher Memminger, Carl Sandburg would produce more than a third of his life work on the farm in his remaining 22 years and win another Pulitzer Prize, this time for poetry.

Henderson County

Phone Number
- (828) 693-4178

Website
- nps.gov/carl

Admission Fee
- None for the grounds; small fee for a tour of the house

Park Hours
- Grounds, sunrise to sunset

Directions
- *Flat Rock*; take Exit 53 off I-26 onto Upward Road west. At its end turn left on Greenville Highway and right on Little River Road to the parking area on the left.

The Walks

On over five miles of groomed hiking trails the Carl Sandburg Home offers something for any level of canine hiker. For easy jaunts with your dog there is a splendid undulating trail around the picturesque Front Lake beneath the house - go around three times for 1.2 miles. For more spirited canine hiking there is a 623-foot climb in 1.5 miles to the views atop the Big Glassy Mountain rockface. Halfway up the mountain, exactly when your panting dog will welcome a breather is a dammed creek reservoir that forms an ideal canine swimming hole. It that hike sounds a bit too ominous you can content yourself with a trip around Little Glassy Mountain on the *Memminger Trail*. And if athletic dogs are whimpering for more, you can abort the trip around and go over the summit of 2,426-foot Little Glassy Mountain that abounds with Lady Slipper's orchids in the spring.

Trail Sense: Superb trail maps are posted and trails well-marked.

Dog Friendliness

Dogs are welcome to trot around the historic Connemara Farm, except in the dairy goat barn.

Traffic

Foot traffic only.

Canine Swimming

Trout Pond is waiting at the base of the Big Glassy Mountain to refresh your dog.

Trail Time

Several hours of canine hiking here.

9
Turkeypen Gap

The Park

Cherokee Indians once used this valley to round up wild turkeys, hence its enduring moniker. In the 1930s the U.S. Forest Service set aside lands where sportsmen in groups of 25 hunted big game for an entire week in primitive areas from wilderness camps, one of which was located here along Cantrell Creek. All provisions and equipment were packed in on a five-mile hike. After that the hunters were on their own with the only restriction being a limit of one deer or bear per hunter.

The Walks

Despite access only via a narrow, vicious dirt road the Turkeypen Gap trails get plenty of play from the horse and bike crowd and canine hikers after long, scenic treks. From the trailhead you make your way downhill to the lively waters of the South Mills River either via a steady trail to the left of the information board or a wide serpentine service road that curves down to the riverbed. The clear, green waters will delight your water-loving dog but they do present an obstacle to the trail system - there are more than a dozen water crossings along the 12-mile *South Mills Trail* and only a pair of swaying suspension

Henderson County

Phone Number
- (828) 877-3265

Website
- fs.usda.gov/nfsnc

Admission Fee
- None

Park Hours
- Sunrise to sunset

Directions
- *Pisgah National Forest*; take Exit 40 off I-26 west towards Brevard on NC 280. Pass through Mill Springs and after passing Brickyard Road on your left look for Turkeypen Road on your right, around the bend of a hill, Turn right and drive 1.25 rough miles to the trailhead.

There are many crossings of South Mills River but only two loosey-goosey bridges.

footbridges that will will put a halt in even the most confident trail dog's step. Expect at least two feet of water in these equestrian fords most times of year. Once on the other side, big canine hiking loops await - and even more water traverses on the *Pounding Mill Trail*, with rocks this time.

Another popular loop for your dog is up the *Turkey Pen Gap Trail* from the left of the parking area which heads across 3,323-foot Sharpy Mountain. The initial pull is the toughest so don't despair in the early going. After that a rollercoaster ridge walk (winter views only) leads to the Wagon Road Gap where a satsfying canine hike can be closed with the *South Mills Trail*.

Trail Sense: There is an information board and signs at the many trail junctions but a map in hand is a must at Turkeypen Gap.

Dog Friendliness
Dogs are allowed on the trails and in the primitive campground.

Traffic
The parking area can fill on a great summer weekend.

Canine Swimming
Your water-loving dog is likely to spend as much time in the pools of the South Mills River as on the trail.

Trail Time
You can sample Turkeypen and not the cross the South Mills River with your dog by linking the two approaches, which with swimming time, creates a worthy 45-minute canine hike. Otherwise plan for at least two hours on any excursion here.

10
Mount Mitchell State Park

The Park

Until Thomas Jefferson made the Louisiana Purchase in 1803 this was the tallest mountain in America, although no one knew it. Everyone assumed Grandfather Mountain was the regional highpoint but after an excursion to the Black Mountains in 1835 a science professor at the University of North Carolina began making claims to the contrary. Using barometric pressure readings and mathematical formulas, Mitchell pegged the elevation at 6,672 - only 12 feet short of today's accepted height. But a controversy arose in the 1850s sparked by Congressman Thomas Clingman who claimed Mitchell had never measured the big peak. The 64-year old scientist trekked back to the mountain in 1857 where he fell from a cliff above a 40-foot waterfall and died. The next year the highest peak east of the Mississippi River was named in his honor. In 1915, with its burly flanks mostly stripped of forest by aggressive logging, Mount Mitchell was established as North Carolina's first state park.

Yancey County

Phone Number
- (828) 675-4611

Website
- ncparks.gov/Visit/parks/momi

Admission Fee
- None

Park Hours
- Opens at 8:00 a.m. with seasonal closing times through the year

Directions
- *Blue Ridge Parkway*; Milepost 355.

The Walks

There are several ways for your dog to tag the Mount Mitchell summit, including the 280-yard walk to the observation deck from the parking lot atop the mountain. The stoutest approach originates from 5.7 miles away and 3,200 feet below in the Black Mountain Campground. Most canine hikers will opt for a middling ascent along the *Old Mitchell Trail* two miles from the Park Office or from the restaurant .7-miles closer. Even at these reduced distances your dog's four-wheel drive will come in handy as you are ascending straight uphill through a lush spruce-fir forest that is fed by an average snowpack of 104 inches per year. Expect the trail to be wet under paw most times you visit.

For experienced canine hikers Mount Mitchell is not the prize but the jumping off point for grander adventures. Although it has 16 peaks over 6,000 feet in height and six of the ten highest in the eastern United States, the hook-shaped Black Mountain range is only 15 miles long. Setting off on the *Deep Gap Trail* from

Clear days like this are rare on Mount Mitchell where the summit is shrouded in mist eight days out of ten.

the summit parking lot your dog can tag four of them before reaching Deep Gap 4.3 miles away. If that is too ambitious a day hike Mt. Craig, named for Governor Locke Craig who spearheaded the creation on the park, is only a two-mile round trip out and back. At 6,647 feet it is the eastern United States' second-highest peak with loads of exposed rock that make it more view-friendly than its slightly loftier neighbor.

Trail Sense: There are signs and maps everywhere on Mount Mitchell - the Park Service doesn't want anyone getting lost up here.

Dog Friendliness
Dogs are welcome everywhere except in the buildings.
Traffic
Foot traffic only on the trails.
Canine Swimming
None.
Trail Time
A few minutes to a full day.

II
Craggy Gardens Recreation Area

The Park

No self-respecting guide to the 469-mile Blue Ridge Parkway ever leaves out the Craggy Gardens. The heath balds blanketed with gnarly rhododendrons have been bandied about for inclusion as one of the country's 600 National Natural Landmarks for their bio-diversity and geological splendor, although they have not yet been so designated (only Mount Mitchell has achieved such rarified status in the Asheville region). The pink and purple floral displays are at their most spectacular in June and July but the head-turning views from Tennessee to central North Carolina make this a favored Parkway stop any time of the year.

Buncombe County

Phone Number
- (828) 298-0358

Website
- nps.gov/blri

Admission Fee
- None

Park Hours
- Sunrise to sundown although Parkway access closes in winter

Directions
- *Blue Ridge Parkway*; Mileposts 363-367.

The Walks

You can immerse your dog in the Craggy Gardens on a set of well-engineered trails around the slopes and mountaintops of the Great Craggy Mountains. The quickest way is through the rhododendron tunnels of the *Craggy Pinnacle Trail* on the way to 360-degree views from the 5,892-foot summit about 3/4 of a mile away. This trail, which leaves from the Craggy Dome Parking Overlook serves up west-facing vistas along the way and can be conquered by even a novice trail dog.

South of the Visitor Center the *Craggy Gardens Trail* kicks off another exploration suitable for any level of canine hiker. The first ten minutes comprise a self-guided nature trail before a side path exits the trees, twisted arboreal warriors in a constant battle with strong winds and winter ice storms, and leads to grassy open meadows and unobstructed views. The path eventually descends to the Picnic Area on the *Mountains-to-Sea-Trail* in another half-mile to add a little bite to your dog's hiking day in the Craggy Gardens. Athletic dogs will want to pick up the *Douglas Falls Trail* just south of the Visitor Center which leads 4.2 strenuous miles through hemlock groves and across racing cascades (be very careful) to the 70-foot freefall of Douglas Creek over a wide rock face.

Trail Sense: Grab a special Craggy Gardens handout.

Your dog can soak in some of the most famous views on the Blue Ridge Parkway at Craggy Gardens.

Dog Friendliness
Dogs can hike these well-trod trails.

Traffic
Foot traffic only.

Canine Swimming
None, not even at Douglas Falls.

Trail Time
Plan on spending at least two hours with your dog in the Gardens.

12
Biltmore House & Gardens

The Park

Cornelius Vanderbilt began his career working on his father's ferry in New York harbor in 1805. When he died in 1877 after a career in shipping and railroading the Commodore was the wealthiest man in America and the richest man ever to die. He had been a bit of a tightwad himself but his descendants knew how to spend money. After a trip to western North Carolina in 1888 when he was 26 grandson George William Vanderbilt decided to build a country home. He began buying land and stopped when he had 125,000 acres. He hired Richard Morris Hunt, the first American to be admitted to the École des Beaux-Arts in Paris – the finest school of architecture in the world, to design a French Renaissance chateau. When the 250-room Biltmore was completed in 1895 it was - and remains - the largest privately owned home in the United States. Vanderbilt's only child, Cornelia Stuyvesant Vanderbilt, opened Biltmore House to the public in 1930; family members continued to live here until 1956, when it was permanently opened to the public as a house museum.

> **Buncombe County**
>
> **Phone Number**
> - 1-877-BILTMORE
>
> **Website**
> - biltmore.com
>
> **Admission Fee**
> - Yes, currently the least expensive access is $35; annual passes start at $129
>
> **Park Hours**
> - Grounds, 9:00 a.m. to dusk
>
> **Directions**
> - *Asheville*; at 1 Lodge Street. Take Exit 50 from I-40 onto US 25 North and follow signs.

The Walks

Outside the exuberant castle is an 8,000-acre estate that includes a forest, a farm, a winery and gardens designed by Frederick Law Olmsted, the chief creator of New York's Central Park and the most influential landscape architect of the 19th century. Your dog is permitted to explore just about everywhere that isn't a building. The paths wind gently down a sloping mountainside from the mansion to the Boat House and Bass Pond, passing through 75 acres of formal gardens, a naturalistic woodland and meadow plantings. Covering these serpentine trails is likely to whet any dog's hiking appetite but if not you can take off on a paved bike path or bridle trail that winds around the grounds. You can hike for days with your dog at Biltmore and never realize

Relaxing on the front lawn of America's largest house.

you are in the backyard of America's largest house.

Trail Sense: A park map will help if you lose sight of the house.

Dog Friendliness
Biltmore is as dog-friendly as any house museum in the country.
Traffic
Depending on where you roam you can encounter bicycles and horses.
Canine Swimming
Your dog can slip into Bass Pond for refreshment.
Trail Time
Take the full day on your visit to Billtmore.

13
Holmes Educational State Forest

The Park

Holmes State Forest, named for John Simcox Holmes who became North Carolina's first State Forester and State Forest Warden in 1915, was created during the Great Depression of the 1930s. The Civilian Conservation Corps, nicknamed "Roosevelt's Tree Army," established a seedling nursery here for many of the 15 million trees that were planted in the state between 1933 and 1938. This was Holmes State Park until 1973 when North Carolina included the park in its new Small State Forest System as "a supplement to the state park system with the primary mission of explaining the forest and forestry." Renamed "educational forests," today North Carolina boast six such properties and the 235-acre Holmes tract is the westernmost.

Henderson County

Phone Number
- (828) 692-0100

Website
- ncesf.org/HESF

Admission Fee
- None

Park Hours
- Gated entrance; 9:00 a.m. to 5:00 p.m. Tuesday-Friday; 10:00 a.m. to 6:00 p.m. Saturday-Sunday; closed Mondays and from the Friday before Thanksgiving to mid-March.

Directions
- *Hendersonville*; at 1299 Crab Creek Road. From I-26 take Exit 49B onto NC 64. In town, turn left on Church Street. At the 8th timed light turn right on Kanuga Road; follow Kanuga Road, which becomes Crab Creek Road, approximately 8.5 miles to the forest entrance on the left.

The Walks

There is something on the hiking menu in Holmes Forest to satisfy any level of trail dog. Looking for a leg-stretcher for a novice canine hiker? The *Crab Creek Trail* moves easily around the parking and picnic areas along the meanderings of Crab Creek for a half-mile. For an appetizer, follow the *Talking Tree Trail* as it slides across the lower slopes surrounding the Forestry Center. Athletic dogs will want to tackle the 3.5-mile *Demonstration Trail* that makes a steep 400-foot ascent before mellowing out and evolving into a first-rate ramble as it swings along the slopes. Along the way various forest management practices are explained. The steepest trail in the forest is the half-mile *Wildcat Rock Trail* that picks it way up outcroppings of granite gneiss that is speckled with shiny flecks of mica. The *Wildcat Rock Trail* can be combined with the *Demonstration Trail* to form a sporty one-hour loop for your dog - take it clockwise to come down Wildcat Rock.

Trail Sense: There are trail map brochures online and on site; there are information boards and the trails are well-marked.

Dog Friendliness

Dogs are allowed to hike the trails in Holmes Forest.

Traffic

Foot traffic only and typically not much of it.

Canine Swimming

Crab Creek is generally deep enough only for splashing. There is a forest pond about half-way into the *Demonstration Trail*, perfectly placed after your dog's greatest exertions.

Trail Time

One to two hours.

A retired North Carolina Forestry Service helicopter is on display in the forest.

14
Richmond Hill
Park

The Park

Richmond Pearson, U. S. Congressman and diplomat, was born on January 26, 1852, in Yadkin County, the fourth of five children of Richmond Pearson, Chief Justice of the North Carolina Supreme Court; both his grandfathers were United States senators. The family land here covered 820 acres, upon which Pearson constructed a grand mansion in 1889, considered one of the most elegant and innovative buildings of its time. Plans were drawn up by James G. Hill, a one-time Supervising Architect for the United States Treasury. Today 183 acres of the former Pearson estate is preserved as Richmond Hill Park, Asheville's largest city park.

Buncombe County

Phone Number
- (828) 259-5800

Website
- ashevillenc.gov/Departments/ParksRecreation

Admission Fee
- None

Park Hours
- Sunrise to sunset

Directions
- *Asheville*; at 280 Richmond Hill Drive. From I-26 take Exit 25 and pick up Riverside Drive south. Turn right and cross the French Broad River on Pearson Bridge Road. Climbing the hill, after the road bends left make a hard right onto Richmond Hill Drive and follow it to its end at the park.

The Walks

Hiking with your dog along the Richmond Hill trail system is akin to moving around a giant model railroad layout. Trail sections pass next to one another and intersect often - there are three sets of blazes and you will see yellow and blue and red blazes throughout your dog's journey here. The marquee canine hike on Richmond Hill is the *Yellow Loop* that motors up and down the slopes, sweeps by the French Broad River three times and makes several stream crossings. Encased completely in a mixed-hardwood forest on paw-friendly footpaths, this is a thoroughly enjoyable 2.75-mile ramble for your dog. The red blazes all leave and come back to the *Yellow Loop* which will add spice to your dog's Richmond Hill experience when

44

you return. The trail system, designed by the Southern Off-Road Bicycle Association, sports its share of tight turns and ups and downs as your dog trots along.

Trail Sense: For your first outing find the yellow blazes and stick with them; the loop goes either left or straight at the information kiosk and crosses the disc golf course where players yell "Disc" not "Fore."

The upper reaches of Richmond Hill Park are blanketed with running pine which, although it resembles a miniature conifer forest, is actually a spore-bearing moss.

Dog Friendliness
Dogs are welcome on the Richmond Hill trails and the disc golf course - and many park users come with a dog in tow.

Traffic
The trails are designed for both mountain bike and foot traffic.

Canine Swimming
The streams that flow through the property are only deep enough for doggie splashin' and sittin'.

Trail Time
One to two hours.

15
Graveyard Fields

The Park

The graveyard in question is not a repository of human remains but rather refers to an ancient windstorm that uprooted the spruce forest that once grew here, leaving behind tree stumps that settlers hundreds of years later reckoned looked like a graveyard. Or maybe it was the feverish logging in the area that left moss-draped tree stumps that resembled weathered tombstones. Or maybe it was the 1925 fire that charred 25,000 acres of timberland that burned hot enough to sterilize the soil. Whatever the origin

Haywood County

Phone Number
- (828) 298-0358

Website
- nps.gov/blri

Admission Fee
- None

Park Hours
- Sunrise to sundown although Parkway access closes in winter

Directions
- *Blue Ridge Parkway*, Milepost 418.8.

of the name the tree-challenged flat mountain valley has been likened to an "upside-down bald" that is unlike anything else along the Blue Ridge Parkway. And not many travelers drive by without stopping - in the summer the cooling waters of three waterfalls on the Yellowstone Prong are the drawing card, in autumn some of North Carolina's best color is seen at Graveyard Fields.

The Walks

This is likely to be among the most "social" canine hikes you take on the Parkway. Steps and an asphalt path lead down through rhododendron thickets to the Yellowstone Prong, which earns its name honestly from the mineral-streaked rocks it flows over. Most people bear right and make for Second Falls but a superior hike with your dog awaits to the left, towards Upper Falls. Mostly flat until the approach to the falls, the route travels through mountain bogs, wetlands and shrub where wild blueberries and blackberries can be gobbled by the handful in the late summer. The loop between the two falls closes and returns to the parking area in about three miles.

More spirited canine hiking awaits beyond the Yellowstone Prong Valley by climbing to *Graveyard Ridge Trail* where a loop can be joined with the *Mountains to Sea Trail* as it passes by. For a full day of hiking with your dog you can climb all the way to the grassy summits of Black Balsam Knob and Tennent Mountain.

The plunge pool at Second Falls makes a dandy canine swimming hole.

Trail Sense: Signs lead you down and through Graveyard Fields; if you want to extend your dog's hiking day and don't have a map you can look around and see where you are.

Dog Friendliness
Dogs are welcome to join the fun in Graveyard Fields.

Traffic
This is a popular spot but the crowds that congregate at Second Falls don't often hike beyond.

Canine Swimming
There is superb dog paddling at the ready along Yellowstone Prong - your dog can even find a sandy beach.

Trail Time
Between one and two hours; more if you hike out of the valley.

16
Davidson River Recreation Area

The Park

Davidson River Recreation Area is one of only two campgrounds in Pisgah National Forest to remain open all year and is by far the largest with 160 sites, more than one-third of all the sites in the forest. You will never find a more accessible campground in a national forest and you don't have to stay in the campground to enjoy its many trails - there are separate parking lots for trail users.

The Walks

Despite the popularity of Davidson River Campground, there is ample opportunity to leave the crowds behind with your dog. The *Art Loeb Trail*, which begins its 30-mile run to Cold Mountain on an agreeably level carriage path beside the river, soon climbs aggressively up and over High Knob, leaving the campground a near, yet distant, memory. (Looking for an easy ramble with your dog? Continue past the *Art Loeb* junction onto the *Estatoe Path* to US 64 and return). You can craft a canine hiking loop of several hours by returning via the *North Slope Connector* or shave time by using FR 5002 back down that deposits you in the center of the campground. The North Slope Ridge is explored on its own four-mile trail launching from a trailhead just before the campsites; it slices across the ridge in addition to traversing it, using the Davidson River as a connector. Depending on your tolerance for communal dog-walking, you can also set your dog to trotting on the camp *Exercise Trail* that moves in lockstep with the crystal clear waters of the Davidson River.

Transylvania County
Phone Number
- (828) 877-3265
Website
- fs.usda.gov/nfsnc
Admission Fee
- None
Park Hours
- Sunrise to sunset
Directions
- *Pisgah National Forest*; east of Brevard at the intersections of US 64, US 276 and NC 280 take US 276 north for 1.1 miles to the campground on the left. Trail parking is on the left, immediately after you make the turn (all paved).

One of the best, easily reached 90-minute canine hiking loops in Pisgah Forest is across US 276 from the campground, next to the maintenance works. Start on the *Black Mountain Trail* and follow it up the slope beside a lushly vegetated stream, keeping an eye out on the left for a small grotto where you dog will happily splash under a tiny waterspout. Veer off onto the *Thrift Cove Trail* where you will soon follow a wide, twisting road back - it is an easier hike doing the loop counterclockwise up this road but you sacrifice the long views into the cove. You can double your dog's good times here with a loop through Sycamore Cove that starts on *Grassy Road* where the trails clang together in a jumble near the bottom.

Wild grasses dominate the open areas of North Slope Ridge above the campground.

Trail Sense: There are a slurry of forest roads and trails around the campground so study a map, although you can manage without.

Dog Friendliness
Dogs are allowed on the trails and in the campground.

Traffic
Except for the *Art Loeb Trail*, you will be sharing these paths with bikes.

Canine Swimming
Look out tubers, I'm coming in - the Davidson River is a swimming dog's paradise.

Trail Time
You could fill a weekend of hiking with your dog during a stay in the Davidson River Campground.

17
Chimney Rock State Park

The Park

The magnificent scenery on display at Hickory Rock Gorge is the combined efforts of man and nature. Nature has been fiddling with the stonework, including the famous 315-foot monolith watching over the valley, for about 535 million years but Lake Lure is the relatively recent handiwork of Lucius B. Morse, a Missouri doctor who first came here in the late 1800s for the fresh air to calm his tuberculosis. Morse wound up buying 64 acres of Chimney Rock for $5,000 in 1902. It was already a tourist destination as original owner Rome Freeman had built a stairway to the top of the rock in 1885. Morse had a grander vision - he would dam the Rocky Broad River and create Lake Lure from which would spring a fabulous resort. The lake was ready by 1927 but the stock market crash two years later and scuttled most of the resort development. Chimney Rock carried on as its own attraction, however, and remained a private park until the Morse family sold it to the State for $24 million in 2007 as the centerpiece for a new state park.

Rutherford County

Phone Number
- (828) 625-9611

Website
- chimneyrockpark.com

Admission Fee
- Yes, varies by season

Park Hours
- 8:30 a.m. - 5:30 p.m DST; shorter hours at other times

Directions
- *Chimney Rock*; at 431 Main Street. Take US 74 from I-40 and Asheville or US 64 from I-26 and Hendersonville or NC 9 from I-40 and Black Mountain.

The Walks

Your dog is encouraged to experience the same wonders as the wide-eyed tourists at Chimney Rock. There is the climb up 500 or so steps to the 75-mile views down and across Lake Lure awaiting atop the rock. There is the further climbing (an elevation gain of 150 feet in a bit more than a half-mile) to the highest point in the park via the *Skyline Trail* to Exclamation Point and its west-facing views up the Gorge. And there is the easy forest ramble to the base of the 404-foot Hickory Nut Falls where your dog can frolic in the plunge pool. This is not the out-in-the-woods-alone-with-your-dog canine hiking you are used to in the mountains around Asheville but well worth the change of pace. If, however, you do want to slip away from the

Your dog will earn his rest after climbing 500 steps to the top of Chimney Rock.

crowds, park below Chimney Rock and set off with your dog on the *Four Seasons Trail* up to the attractions less than a mile away.

Trail Sense: Signs and maps lead the way to the park attractions.

Dog Friendliness
The Chimney Rock brochure proclaims "We Love Dogs" - take them at their word.

Traffic
Foot traffic only - and busy most of the year.

Canine Swimming
The water under Hickory Nut Falls is deep enough for small dogs.

Trail Time
Allow two-to-three hours to fully explore Chimney Rock with your dog.

18
North Carolina Arboretum

The Park

Frederick Law Olmsted is recognized as the founder of American landscape architecture and the nation's foremost parkmaker. Olmsted's genius shaped the cities of New York (Central Park), Boston (Emerald Necklace) and Montreal (Mount Royal Park) among scores of others. His last major project was George William Vanderbilt's Biltmore Estate, which Olmsted laid out while in his seventies. He died before his dream of establishing a arboretum on the grounds could be realized. Olmsted's vision did not begin taking shape until the 1980s when 426 acres in the Pisgah National Forest were allocated for a true plant museum. In the 1990s the first gardens dedicated to the Southern Appalachian region were installed.

Buncombe County

Phone Number
- (828) 665-2492

Website
- ncarboretum.org

Admission Fee
- Parking fee except for the first Tuesday of every month; you can also hike in from the Lake Powhatan Recreation Area

Park Hours
- 8:00 a.m. to 7/9:00 p.m.

Directions
- *Asheville*; Milepost 393 of the Blue Ridge Parkway or Exit 33 off I-26, two miles south on US 191.

The Walks

You aren't likely to take a prettier hike with your dog in the Blue Ridge than in the North Carolina Arboretum, whether it be through wildflowers or planted gardens. Eventually the groomed woodland paths will land canine hikers on the *Bent Creek Road*, a wide, flat multi-purpose artery that hugs the gentle meanderings of Bent Creek. If the traffic is heavy you can lead your dog onto the dirt footpaths that occasionally slip between the road and the creek. Not to be missed is the maze of short paths that wander through the National Native Azalea Collection that decorate the floodplain from March to August with 16 of the 17 azalea species native to the United States. All of the canine hiking around Bent Creek is easy going. If you are hiking into the Arboretum from Lake Powhatan Recreation Area, this is the road/trail you are on when you go through the chain link gate.

For dogs looking for a sportier hiking day in the North Carolina Arboretum depart Bent Creek and climb the _Rocky Cove Road_ or _Hard Times Road_

Your dog won't be in a hurry to race through the trails of the North Carolina Arboretum.

which are linked by the one-mile, pine-scented _Owl Ridge Trail_ to form a splendid loop. The roads link outside the gates in Pisgah National Forest for an even more challenging canine hike.

Trail Sense: There are paths moving every which way and not all are signed but you shouldn't need to summon the Saint Bernard rescue squad here.

Dog Friendliness
Dogs are permitted on the Arboretum trails but not in all the gardens so pay heed to the signs - there is still plenty of beauty to enjoy with your dog without going everywhere.

Traffic
Bikes are plentiful on Bent Creek Road.

Canine Swimming
Bent Creek is great for splashing on a hot day but seldom pools deep enough for dog paddling.

Trail Time
At least an hour and several more possible.

19
Coontree
Picnic Area

The Park

The Pisgah National Forest was established in 1916, using some of the first funds from the Weeks Act that was signed into federal law in 1911 to provide $9 million for the conservation and purchase of six million acres of land in the eastern United States. Coontree Picnic Area is in the core of the original lands comprising Pisgah Forest and is a popular stopping place for families and those looking to play in the Davidson River - most of whom are unaware of the hiking loop across US 276. Coontree is also conveniently located near two of the most popular

Transylvania County

Phone Number
- (828) 877-3265

Website
- fs.usda.gov/nfsnc

Admission Fee
- None

Park Hours
- Sunrise to sunset

Directions
- *Pisgah National Forest*; east of Brevard at the intersections of US 64, US 276 and NC 280 take US 276 north for 4.7 miles to the picnic grounds on the left.

single-trail trailheads in Pisgah Forest - one an iconic lookout and the other a plunging, walk-behind waterfall.

The Walks

Coontree Loop. This loop is created by two fingers of trail that diverge from Coontree Creek and climb to the ridge and *Bennett Gap Trail*. To the north, your left, the path continues across Coontree Mountain and down into Saddle Gap where views can be stolen through the trees east and west (including Looking Glass Rock). Most canine hikers seem to take the *Coontree Loop* in a counterclockwise direction, saving the western finger, that is more of a pick-your-way hiking path, for the downhill leg of the 3.5-mile loop but there doesn't seem an advantage either way.

Looking Glass Rock Trail. Just north of Coontree Picnic Area, Forest Road 475 heads west and quickly reaches the normally busy trailhead for the 3.1-mile trek up Looking Glass Rock, the most recognizable landmark of Pisgah Forest. Geologists call the ball of granite a pluton that would have become a volcano if it hadn't cooled so fast. Rising to 3,969 feet, it takes its name from the rainwater that freezes on its surface and reflects the sun like a mirror. It is a steady climb to be sure but unlikely to bring your dog to her knees. Nearing the top you will pass a flat spot in the crown emblazoned with a painted

The top of Looking Glass Rock.

white "H" where helicopters land to rescue injured climbers. As well as a good place to gather for your final push to the summit, a spur trail here leads to viewpoints on Lower Looking Glass Cliffs . Once on the exposed rock face don't get greedy with your views - your dog can see just fine from the edge of the woods, thank you.

Moore Cove Falls Trail. A short way up US 276 you will reach the parking area at Looking Glass Creek for Moore Cove Falls. The well-engineered trail runs .7-mile through a pretty stretch of forest to where the water spills over a jutting rock ledge.

Trail Sense: The trails are well-signed.

Dog Friendliness
Dogs are allowed on these three trails.

Traffic
Foot traffic only.

Canine Swimming
The streams on all these trails are of the splashing variety.

Trail Time
A full day for all three.

20
Bent Creek Experimental Forest

The Park

European settlers moving into the area in the late 1700s named this creek for a horseshoe-shaped bend near the French Broad River. Over the next hundred years the entire area was logged and bustled with more than 100 homes and 20 businesses. After the Forest Service purchased this land it set aside 1,100 acres around Bent Creek for research by the Appalachian Forest Experiment Station, which Congress had established in 1921 as one of the oldest experimental forests in the East. In 1935, about 5,200 acres were added and the Experimental Forest now includes most of the Bent Creek Watershed. In 1942 the creek was dammed and the 13-acre Lake Powhatan formed to become the center for recreational activity in the forest.

Buncombe County

Phone Number
- (828) 257-4832

Website
- srs.fs.usda.gov/bentcreek

Admission Fee
- None

Park Hours
- Sunrise to sunset

Directions
- *Pisgah National Forest*; from I-26 take Exit 33 and go 1.8 miles south to Wesley Branch Road on the right. Turn and follow into the forest and the information board on the right (all paved).

The Walks

There are no great destinations in Bent Creek Forest, no spectacular waterfalls, no awe-inspiring views. What there is, however, is great woods-walking with your dog on gated jeep roads and foot trails that ease you up the slopes on long, sinuous hikes. Bent Creek and its 44 miles of trails is not the place to come for a quick leg-stretcher. Your dog will find the easiest trotting around Lake Powhatan and down beside Bent Creek (and plenty of company on the trails as well.) These stream-bottom communities are thick with rhododendron and stands of white pine and hemlock which thin out the further you venture up the slopes. One of the best hiking loops with your dog without driving too deep into the forest is up the Ledyard and Wolf branches north of Lake Powhatan. In the course of almost five miles you pass through fern-encrusted clearcuts, regenerating hardwood forests and selected harvest plots.

Trail Sense: Unlike other areas of the vast Pisgah National Forest, printed trail maps can be had for Bent Creek Experimental Forest both from information centers and online.

Bent Creek is a fine place to cool your dog's paws after a long hike in the woods.

Dog Friendliness
Dogs are allowed on the trails and in the campground but not in Lake Powhatan and not on the beach.

Traffic
The extensive trail system is a magnet for mountain bikers and only a few of the trails are hiker-only.

Canine Swimming
Dogs can't swim in Lake Powhatan and the surrounding streams seldom pool deep enough for anything but the smallest dogs to swim.

Trail Time
On most any trail you set off on with your dog in Bent Creek Forest don't expect to return for at least an hour.

21
Green River Game Lands

The Park

The Environmental and Conservation Organization began in the early 1990s as a hiking group and has evolved into stewards of the natural heritage of the Carolina mountains. They are responsible for the creation of 16 miles of trails through an undeveloped wilderness of 10,000 acres known as the Green River Game Lands. Owned by the state, hunting is what these lands are all about. But there is no hunting on Sundays and most of the summer, so there is plenty of opportunity for a safe canine hike.

The Walks

You say you want to disappear with your dog into the woods? You've come to the right place. This is an undisturbed land of steep ravines, plunging waters and towering trees. The trail system is a blend of abandoned jeep roads and footrails and much of untamed Green River can be overgrown

Henderson County

Phone Number
- (828) 692-0385

Website
- eco-wnc.org

Admission Fee
- None

Park Hours
- Sunrise to sunset

Directions
- *Saluda*; from I-26 take Exit 53 east on Upward Road. After 1.8 miles turn right on Big Hungry Road that bends left and right. After twisting down to the river, there are unmarked trailheads at 2.0 miles, 2.4 miles and 2.9 miles on the right. For the Green Cove River Trail take Exit 59 off I-26. On the east side of the highway turn left on Green River Cove Road. After many hairpins down you reach the river; continue across the river past a tube rental place and park on the right across the bridge. The obscured trailhead is across the street, to the left of the driveway.

and downright indecipherable in places - starting with the trailheads. The brown trailhead markers are placed several yards into the trails and not visible from the road. Even following the exacting directions in the excellent park brochure (available only at area tourist centers) can leave you scratching your head. The two main trails penetrating Green River are the scenic 3.25-mile *Pulliam Creek Trail* from the Big Hungry Road and the *Green River Cove*

Trail, a splendid canine ramble that traces the river for over three miles. Both are out-and-back affairs, unless your dog is up for some bushwhacking and you try to create hiking loops with map firmly in hand. Most of the time you will be moving up or down but seldom will the ascents set your dog to serious panting, save for a nearly vertical drop from the *Pulliam Creek Trail* down to the Green River and the Narrows, which is not advised. Better to access the end of the Narrows from the *Green River Cove Trail.* The *Long Ridge Trail* makes a particularly pleasing ascent on a twisting jeep road for two miles into the forest.

Trail Sense: The trails are unblazed; there are some markers at junctions but find a map before coming to Green River.

Dog Friendliness
There are no restrictions on dogs at Green River.

Traffic
Foot traffic only - and little of it most days.

Canine Swimming
There are places along the *Green River Cove Trail* where your dog can slip in and paddle with the tubers. A half-mile down the *Bishop Branch Trail* there is a splendid doggie swimming hole under a small waterfall. There is grand dog paddling in the Big Hungry River below the dam as well.

Trail Time
At least an hour to a half-day.

This waterfall on the Bear Branch Trail makes for an ideal doggie swimming hole.

22

Cove Creek Falls/ Daniel Ridge Falls

The Park

These are the green expanses of trees one sees when viewing Looking Glass Rock from the Blue Ridge Parkway. Whereas the emphasis on much of the canine hiking west of US 276 in the Pisgah National Forest is on views, here the attraction is water. The Davidson River begins up in these ridges and puts forth a wholly different visage than its downstream appearance along the roadway.

The Walks

Where the paved section of FS 475 ends and the gravel begins are two loop trails whose main lure are waterfalls: Cove Creek and Daniel Ridge. The tumbling waters are actually near their respective trailheads and chances are if you take the full loops beyond the falls with your dog you will have forgotten them by the time you return to your car, so transcendent is the beauty of the woodlands.

Cove Creek Falls are located on a 5-mile loop that includes Caney Bottom Creek to the east. Cascades and hidden pools on both streams your dog will love conspire to lessen the impact of the big-name falls, which are reached by descending off the main trail. Above the falls, *Cove Creek Trail* flexes its muscles as it stretches across the valley

Transylvania County

Phone Number
- (828) 877-3265

Website
- fs.usda.gov/nfsnc

Admission Fee
- None

Park Hours
- Sunrise to sunset

Directions
- *Pisgah National Forest*; from the Visitor Center on US 276 go 3.5 miles north and turn left on FS 475. Go three miles past the Fish Hatchery to parking for Cove Creek Group Camp on the right; parking for Daniel Ridge is one more mile up the road.

Some of Cove Creek's cascades are as enticing for your dog as its falls.

with surrounding views.

Daniel Ridge Falls, which is actually on Tom's Spring and sometimes called Toms Spring Falls or even Jackson Falls, is a 150-foot cascade that clings to a rock-face. It is upstaged on its walk by the energetic, tree-shrouded waters of the Davidson River. There is also an Upper Falls to explore, along Forest Service Road 5046 that

it is tucked deep into a dark, mossy grotto just off the *Daniel Ridge Loop*. If the beguiling open forests along the Davidson River have cast a spell, you can continue exploring up the *Farlow Gap Trail* that goes three often wet and rooty miles across a series of ridges.

Trail Sense: Each of these falls is actually off its trail; the base of Daniel Ridge Falls is 100 yards down the forest road which continues and re-connects back to the *Daniel Ridge Loop*.

Dog Friendliness
Dogs are allowed to hike on these trails.

Traffic
This is a popular mountain biking spot so keep your head on a swivel; no bikes are allowed on the *Caney Bottom Loop*.

Canine Swimming
Some play in the water is never more than a few minutes down the trail.

Trail Time
Allow two to three hours to complete each waterfall loop.

23

Perry N. Rudnick Nature and Public Art Trail

The Park

Perry N. Rudnick owned a printing business in New York City and collected sculpture. After retiring to Laurel Park in 1982 he fell under the spell of the Blue Ridge Mountains and traded his sedentary lifestyle for not only hiking trails but building them. By 1985 he had earned a certificate of achievement for climbing 40 designated peaks in the Southern Appalachians. In 1989 he was recognized by the United States Forest Service for having logged 10,000 hours of trail maintenance and construction. Before Perry Rudnick passed away at the age of 86 in 2000 he set up a foundation which funded the creation of the *Nature and Public Art Trail* in 2002. The University of North Carolina-Asheville property was once the summer home of Kathryn A. Kellogg, whose husband's fortune came from inventing the switches and electrical circuits built by the Square D (for Detroit) Company in Michigan.

The Walks

The *Rudnick Art Trail* moves peaceably from meadow to hemlock grove to hardwood forest. Ferns and

Henderson County

Phone Number
- (828) 890-2050

Website
- kelloggcenter.org

Admission Fee
- None

Park Hours
- Sunrise to sunset

Directions
- *Hendersonville*; at 1181 Broyles Road. From I-26 take Exit 49B onto NC 64. Continue through town and past Laurel Park. Turn right on Broyles Road and continue to the Kellogg Center on the left. If the gate is closed, continue to Rugby Road and turn left.

trillium often sprout by the soft dirt and grassy footpaths. But of most interest are the 14 public art works on the grounds and trail. The first commissioned piece can be found around a bend in the woodlands here where Harry McDaniel's Fiddleheads wave like elephantine ferns opening is spring. The full tour of both the *North Trail* and the *South Trail* will cover about one mile and is so agreeable your dog is likely to demand touring again.

Trail Sense: Descriptive brochures are available at the trailhead. There are some more footpaths than are shown on the map but you won't get lost if your dog leads you off the *Rudnick Art Trail*.

Dog Friendliness
Dogs are welcome to enjoy the public art at the Kellogg Center.
Traffic
Foot traffic only.
Canine Swimming
The streams that lubricate the trails are only for splashing.
Trail Time
About an hour.

Rudy Rudisill's *The Mother House*, fabricated of steel washed with muriatic acid and coated in wax, is one of 14 works of art found around the Rudnick Art Trail.

24
Mount Pisgah

The Park

The Cherokee Indians who lived here knew this mountain as Elseetoss and the ridge as Warwasseeta. There are conflicting stories of how the rounded summit became named for the biblical mount from which Moses first saw the "promised land" but by 1808 Mount Pisgah was appearing on North Carolina maps. Thomas Lanier Clingman, a U.S. Senator and Confederate General, owned 300 acres around the mountaintop for most of the 19th century until shortly before his death in 1897, when he sold this land to George W. Vanderbilt as part of the 125,000-acre Biltmore estate.

Buncombe County

Phone Number
- (828) 298-0358

Website
- nps.gov/blri

Admission Fee
- None

Park Hours
- Sunrise to sundown although Parkway access closes in winter

Directions
- *Blue Ridge Parkway*; Milepost 407.6.

Vanderbilt constructed a hunting lodge in Buck Springs Gap at the base of Mount Pisgah and carved a trail out from Biltmore for his guests. When Edith Vanderbilt sold 80,000 acres, including Mount Pisgah, to the United States Forest Service in 1914 the family retained 471 acres around the lodge. In 1918 the public began arriving at Mount Pisgah when the batten-board Pisgah Inn opened. It was rebuilt in the 1960s, about the same time the Blue Ridge Parkway was opened for travel here.

The Walks

The narrow footpath to the summit of Mount Pisgah that crosses the Parkway is a familiar trek for Asheville visitors, who can easily see the 5,721-foot peak from downtown. The first half of the 1.6-mile hike to tag the summit moves along agreeably, gaining only about 200 feet in elevation. After a couple of 90-degree right turns, however, the fangs come out with a more-or-less straight uphill 500-foot pull for the last half of this classic canine hike. This is a rock-infested trail with plenty of hops for your dog on both steps and small ledges. Northern red oaks have impeded your view most of the way but at the summit an observation deck serves up views of the Parkway, Cold Mountain to the west and the ever-popular look back at your car in the parking lot.

You can also hike with your dog two miles to the next peak to the south, Frying Pan Mountain (or you can drive to the Forest Service Road 450 at Milepost 409.6) and just walk the final .7 of a mile up a gravelly dirt road to the 5,340-foot summit. Waiting for you at the top is the tallest lookout tower in Western North Carolina - a 70-foot high, five-flight steel structure. This is not a dog-friendly tower with open steps and some rail-less stairs but even one flight will get you high enough for panoramic views.

Back in the Mount Pisgah parking lot you can lead your dog south on a leg-stretcher to the foundations of the historic Vanderbilt hunting lodge that was razed in the 1960s. You can sit in the quiet clearing today and imagine what it was like to own everything you can see.

Trail Sense: No side trails to worry about.

Dog Friendliness
Dogs are allowed on Mount Pisgah.
Traffic
Horses and bikes are not allowed on Blue Ridge Parkway trails.
Canine Swimming
None.
Trail Time
Between two and three hours at George Vanderbilt's old lodge site.

25
Hot Springs Area

The Park

A natural hot spring is located at the confluence of the French Broad River and Spring Creek, the only such spring known to flow in North Carolina. The Cherokee Indians came to the waters for healing and in early America the springs were a popular stopping point for travelers and the Buncombe Turnpike tollroad was run out to Warm Springs, as it was then known, in 1828. For the next 100 years different manifestations of a resort hotel operated here, spreading the fame of the magical healing waters. The last glamorous resort burned in 1920 and the area slid into decline; two subsequent hotels burned and today the 100-degree geothermal springs are privately owned as a spa.

Madison County

Phone Number
- (828) 877-3265

Website
- fs.usda.gov/nfsnc

Admission Fee
- None

Park Hours
- Sunrise to sunset

Directions
- *Pisgah National Forest*; take Exit 19 off I-26 onto US 25/70 north for 28 miles to Hot Springs.

The Walks

The *Appalachian Trail* (AT) passes through Hot Springs and it is well-known as a spot for thru-hikers to take a civilization break and re-supply. The must-do canine hike in Hot Springs is the *Lover's Leap Loop* across French Broad River from the town - you can start your explorations by crossing the bridge or at the Silvermine Trailhead at the base of the rocky ridge. Switchbacks help with the 500-foot elevation gain on the 1.6-mile trail - the longer ones come up from the river side of the hike but you may want to take the steeper route from the trailhead and save the easy mile-long leg along the French Broad for the end. Once on top you will discover the spots from where every photograph you've ever seen of Hot Springs was snapped. A narrow trail leads down to Lovers Leap Rock where a Cherokee maiden supposedly jumped to her death after learning her lover had been slain by a jealous rival - no place for a rambunctious dog but there are equally fabulous views along the ridge.

You can extend your dog's outing in Hot Springs at the Rocky Bluff Campground, three miles down NC 209 (hikers park in picnic area). This is reclaimed cropland and much of your canine hiking here will be on roads through the remains of an old farm - look for foundations, dry-stack stone walls and a family cemetery among the planted pine plantations. The two trails here will both give your dog a spirited hike - the 2.6-mile *Van Cliff Loop Trail* leaves near Campsite #8

Enjoying the view of Hot Springs from the Lovers Leap Trail.

and reaches the boulder-laced ridgetops and the *Spring Creek Nature Trail* from #14 covers about half that distance and climbs only half as high.

Trail Sense: When the white-blazed AT goes up, go down.

Dog Friendliness
Dogs are allowed to hike on these trails.

Traffic
Foot traffic only.

Canine Swimming
The French Broad River is tame enough for a doggie dip most of the time.

Trail Time
Several hours.

26

Crabtree Falls Recreation Area

The Park

When European settlers pushed into this area in the late 1700s they found large swatches of open meadows on the top of the mountains that they chalked up to Indians setting fires to clear the woodlands centuries earlier. The open spaces were once filled with crab apple orchards that are now gone but the meadows remain. Today those meadows are known as a showcase for mountain wildflowers in the summer.

The Walks

The highlight for canine hikers here is Crabtree Creek, an otherwise unremarkable mountain stream until it slides seductively over a 60-foot rock cliff. The hike with your dog to the falls assumes a heavy tourist flavor as you maneuver through a campground and descend 500 feet over a mile with the aid of rock steps and handrails. There is no plunge pool for your dog to play in at Crabtree Falls but the cove is saturated with water spray and spring seeps to cool your best trail companion.

After admiring the rivulets snaking down the rock face, cross the

Yancey County

Phone Number
- (828) 298-0358

Website
- nps.gov/blri

Admission Fee
- None

Park Hours
- Sunrise to sundown although Parkway access closes in winter

Directions
- *Blue Ridge Parkway*; Milepost 339.5.

Where's the plunge pool? your water-loving dog is likely to wonder at Crabtree Falls.

Bonus

Spend an hour, spend a day, there is no reason to rush your dog through Blue Ridge Parkway trails - all the nine first-come, first-served campgrounds, including at Crabtree Meadows, on the Parkway welcome dogs.

bridge and continue your canine hike where the trail begins to growl. A series of switchbacks through the mixed oak-hickory forest climb the mountain on the south side of the falls until leveling out on a ridge behind a manufactured rock wall. From here the remainder of the 2.5-mile loop will delight your dog with long, level stretches and stream crossings.

All the campgrounds on the Blue Ridge Parkway are dog-friendly.

Trail Sense: The trail leaves from the parking lot next to the campground entrance booth. If the campground is closed, as it is seasonally from November to mid-April, you will begin at the marked trailhead from the Blue Ridge Parkway lot and hike through the meadow and campground to begin the journey to the falls. You can usually find a trail map at the entrance booth but the *Falls Trail* is well-signed. Also, this is not the Crabtree Picnic Area that is on the opposite side of the Parkway.

Dog Friendliness
Dogs are welcome on the trails and in the campground.
Traffic
Foot traffic only; this is a busy stop on the Parkway although the trail rating as "strenuous" will thin the crowds.
Canine Swimming
Despite being above the Falls, Crabtree Creek is benign enough to form several deep canine swimming pools were dog-paddling is on tap.
Trail Time
Allow between one anf two hours to fully explore Crabtree Falls.

27
Shut-In
Trail

The Park

Many of us have had the experience of building paths around our yards to different features of the property. In the 1890s, for George William Vanderbilt, that meant hacking out a horse trail about 22 miles long to get to his hunting lodge at Mount Pisgah from his house at Biltmore. When the Blue Ridge Parkway was constructed in 1962 engineers followed the route of Vanderbilt's path along the ridge. Some 16 miles of the historic trail, in turn, became today's *Shut-In Trail*, so named because the dense thickets of rhododendron wrapped around trail users. So closely did the Parkway route mirror the original path that you are never more than a half-mile away from "America's Favorite Drive" and its 19 million annual visitors while on the *Shut-In Trail*.

Buncombe County
Phone Number - (828) 298-0358
Website - nps.gov/blri
Admission Fee - None
Park Hours - Sunrise to sundown although Parkway access closes in winter
Directions - *Blue Ridge Parkway*, Mileposts 393.6-407.6.

The Walks

The *Shut-in Trail*, which is now incorporated into the *Mountains to Sea Trail*, has been diced into about a dozen segments as it weaves back and forth across the Blue Ridge Parkway. This affords many options to take advantage of *Shut-In* with your dog. You can use it for quick leg-stretchers from the Parkway overlooks. Or, since it gains 3000 feet in elevation from the French Broad River to Mount Pisgah, almost any trail segment will provide a convenient work-out for your athletic trail companion. If you have multiple vehicles or a pick-up, the *Shut-In Trail* can provide a full day of scenic canine hiking - and don't be dissuaded by the name, most of the trail is through open hardwood forests, not tunnels of rhododendron.

But the best time to trot your dog to the *Shut-In Trail* is in the winter when the barricades go up on the Parkway. Not only are the winter views unforgettable but the deserted roadway can be used to create easy canine hiking loops.

Trail Sense: You won't find the *Shut-In Trail* on any official Blue Ridge Parkway maps but the white dots and signs are easily picked up from the overlooks.

Dog Friendliness
Dogs are welcome on the Blue Ridge Parkway trails.
Traffic
Foot traffic only when you are off the roadway.
Canine Swimming
None.
Trail Time
Less than an hour to a full day.

The only thing better than reveling in the views from your car on the Blue Ridge Parkway is to enjoy them on foot with your dog.

28
Bearwallow Mountain

The Park

Bearwallow Mountain lords over eastern Henderson County at an elevation of 4,232 feet; it is the second-highest point in the county. A grassy meadow summit spilling down its northwest face helps distinguish the peak from its neighbors across the Eastern Continental Divide. The lack of trees enable windspeeds to accelerate to many times that which may be buffering canine hikers at lower elevations, sometimes exceeding 100 mph. Trees that are hundreds of years old are the height of youngsters and in places the wind has scooped out depressions from the thin soil that resemble the bunkers on windsept, seaside Scottish golf courses. With the coming of the communications age Bearwallow was a magnet for tower construction and today the summit is peppered with all manner of electronic apparatus. In 2009, the Carolina Mountain Land Conservancy placed a conservation easement on 81 acres at the top of Bearwallow Mountain with plans to preserve almost another 500.

Henderson County

Phone Number
- (828) 697-5777

Website
- carolinamountain.org

Admission Fee
- None

Park Hours
- Sunrise to sunset

Directions
- *Edneyville*; from I-26 take Exit 49 onto US 64 East and go six miles to Mills Gap Road and turn left. In a quarter-mile turn right on Bearwallow Road. When it ends in 2.5 miles turn left on Old Clear Creek Road and right on Bearwallow Mountain Road. At 2.5 miles bear right - do not go straight on North Bearwallow Road. Parking is on the side of the road in another 2.5 miles when the road turns to gravel. You can also get here by coming up that gravel road from US 74 in Gerton.

The Walks

Here is a chance for your dog to feel the sun on her neck. You have to make your way through airy hardwoods to reach the wide open spaces on Bearwallow Mountain from the trailhead. A well-engineered, switch-backing and stepped footpath battles the 537-foot gain in elevation and in less than a half- hour your dog will be bursting out of the trees into the wide open spaces. The white-diamond blazed trail joins the service road that you will use for your descent at this point but your dog will no doubt want to romp on the grassy hillsides for the short stretch to the top. On clear days the panoramic summit serves up 100-mile views; hopefully you have remembered your binoculars. From the top of the abandoned 47-foot firetower, built in 1937 and decommissioned in 1994 and now off-limits, ten counties could be scanned for forest

When in operation, firespotters could scan ten counties from atop Bearwallow Mountain.

fires - spotting at times dozens a day - but you will have to be content with long views into Asheville and beyond Apple Valley into Hendersonville.

Trail Sense: A mapboard is at the trailhead and easy to decipher; the *Bearwallow Mountain Trail* is marked by white diamonds.

Dog Friendliness
Dogs are welcome on Bearwallow Mountain.

Traffic
Foot traffic only - and those feet may belong to cattle during the summer.

Canine Swimming
None.

Trail Time
About one hour.

29
Mountains-to-Sea Trail

The Park

Conceived in the 1970s by Howard Lee, then Secretary of the North Carolina Department of Natural Resources and Community Development, a coalition of public agencies and private volunteers are attempting to cobble together a hiking path of over 930 miles from Clingman's Dome in the Great Smoky Mountains to Jockey's Ridge on Cape Hatteras, the highest sand dune on the Atlantic Coast. In 1982, a 75.8-mile trail along the Cape Hatteras National Seashore became the first segment of the trail to be dedicated. To date a little more than 500 somewhat disjointed miles of the *Mountains-to-Sea Trail* (MST) have been completed, mostly in the mountains and at the sea. The MST tags the Blue Ridge Parkway for about 300 of its miles and around Asheville the 60 miles of the MST between Mount Mitchell and Mount Pisgah are maintained by the Carolina Mountain Club. This stretch was designated a National Recreation Trail in 2005.

Buncombe County

Phone Number
- (828) 298-0358

Website
- ncmst.org

Admission Fee
- None

Park Hours
- Sunrise to sundown although Parkway access closes in winter

Directions
- *Blue Ridge Parkway*; Visitor Center at Milepost 384.4.

The Walks

The MST hops back and forth across the Blue Ridge Parkway and 30 trail segments have been identified. One of the most convenient places to sample the trail from Asheville is at the Parkway Visitor Center (where a descriptive brochure identifies the 30 trailheads). The MST is across the Parkway from the Visitor Center and a 1.2-mile loop has been created (one of the crossings is under the Parkway through a stone-faced tunnel). The easy going here is a superb introduction to the trail for the novice canine

hiker. You will find more of the same hiking north to the Folk Art Center (2.7 miles) or south to the French Broad River (about 10 miles with access points at the highway overpasses).

Trail Sense: The trail is blazed with white dots; feeder trails are blazed in blue.

Dog Friendliness
Dogs are welcome on the Blue Ridge Parkway trails.
Traffic
Foot traffic only.
Canine Swimming
An occasional small stream crossing.
Trail Time
Anything from a leg-stretcher to a day's outing with your dog.

30
Green Knob
Lookout Tower

The Park

Views. That is what 5,090-foot
Green Knob is all about. Mostly of
the brawny Black Mountain Range,
including Mount Mitchell, the
highest peak east of the Mississippi
River, that you can almost reach out
and touch to the northwest. The
Civilian Conservation Corps built a
lookout tower atop Green Knob in
1932 and, poking above the treeline,
you can see the pyramidal cap traveling from either direction on the Blue
Ridge Parkway. The lookout was
staffed by live-in rangers into the
1970s (you will see power lines on the
mountain) but when it was rendered
obsolete it was fixed up for hikers
rather than torn down.

The Walks

Any level of trail dog can make
it to the Green Knob Lookout
Tower from the Blue Ridge Parkway on a switch-backing half-mile
trail that tackles a 340-foot elevation   gain. From the Green Knob
Overlook walk 100 yards north and
look carefully for the faded yellow
blazes heading up the mountain - this
is a trail less traveled. At the tower

Yancey County

Phone Number
- (828) 298-0358

Website
- nps.gov/blri

Admission Fee
- None

Park Hours
- Sunrise to sundown although
Parkway access closes in winter

Directions
- *Blue Ridge Parkway*;
Milepost 350.4.

**The lookout tower is the canine
hiker's destination on
Green Knob.**

a single flight of wide, open steps leads to the outside deck which your dog can easily negotiate.

But Green Knob can also be the anchor for truly epic canine hikes. From Black Mountain Campground (page 89) a steep and rocky footpath picks its way up Lost Cove Ridge for 2.8 miles to the base of the observation tower. Truly ambitious canine hikers with a car shuttle can park one vehicle at Mount Mitchell and drive back to the Green Knob Overlook. From there it is a half-mile to the summit of Green Knob, 2.8 miles down to the campground and 5.7 miles to the top of Mt. Mitchell. That should slake your dog's thirst for mountain climbing for a day or two.

Trail Sense: There isn't much signage here so if you are going past the lookout tower bring a map.

Dog Friendliness
Dogs can enjoy the views from the Green Knob lookout tower.
Traffic
Foot traffic only.
Canine Swimming
None.
Trail Time
Less than one hour to climb to the tower and return to the Parkway.

31
Pacolet Area Conservancy Trails

The Park

The Pacolet Area Conservancy formed in 1989 to protect and conserve the Pacolet River that rises on the slopes of the Blue Ridge Mountains in southeastern Henderson County and flows through the Foothills region on its journey to the Santee River and the Atlantic Ocean. The conservancy was able to save a hunk of third growth forest on Little Warrior Mountain- it is a testament to the tenacity of the axemen that the steep southern slopes of this 2,408-foot mountain were cleared twice.

The Walks

Conservancy literature describes the three miles of trails through the 185 acres of the Norman Wilder Forest as "an enjoyable moderate hike" but the stacks of wooden hiking sticks piled at the trailhead offer mute testimony to the contrary. Athletic dogs will want to start at the trailhead on Route 176 and climb up a switchbacking road that serves up views across the Pacolet Valley; others can drive to an alternate parking lot up the dirt Tau Rock Vineyard Road. From here the trail system cuts across the mid-point of the mountain but the two park destinations - the Little Warrior Mountain palisades and a seasonal waterfall that trickles over a rock fortress - are each reached with a steep pulls where the descents are more treacherous than the going up. Your dog's four-wheel drive will be as asset on these trails.

Polk County

Phone Number
- (828) 859-5060

Website
- pacolet.org

Admission Fee
- None

Park Hours
- Sunrise to sunset

Directions
- *Tryon*; From I-26 take Exit 67 onto Route 108 westbound towards Tryon. For the Shuford trails take your first left onto Shuford Drive and you will quickly reach the woodlands. Turn right into the small parking area. For the Wilder trails continue on Route 108 and bear right to Route 176 just before Tryon. After crossing the Pacolet River look for the signed parking area on the right.

The Pacolet Area Conservancy also maintains the Weaverbarton Shuford Memorial Wildlife Sanctuary less than a mile from the Columbus/Tryon interchange off I-26. There are no grand destinations here - just a half-hour or so of pleasurable woods walking with your dog on a series of narrow, connecting footpaths. The most striking feature of this woodland are the scores of fallen trees that litter the forest floor, victims of a winter ice storm back in 1993.

Its not unusual to find dogs in the driver seat during the Coon Dog Day parade.

Trail Sense: Trail map brochures are available at the trailheads.

Dog Friendliness
Dogs are welcome on to explore Pacolet Area Conservancy trails.

Traffic
Foot traffic only - and don't expect much of it.

Canine Swimming
Streams contain just enough water for your dog to cool off a bit.

Trail Time
Between one and two hours in the Norman Wilder Forest and less than one hour in Weaverbarton Shuford Memorial Sanctuary.

32
Rattlesnake Lodge

The Park

Chase P. Ambler came to Asheville as a young medical student in the 1890s and his eminence as a physician had much to do with spreading the fame of the town as a resort for health seekers. His passion was the mountains and at his urging the Appalachian National Park Association was formed in 1899. In his role with the organization Ambler was the driving force behind the creation of Great Smoky Mountains National Park, where 6,100-foot Mount Ambler is named in his honor, and the Pisgah National Forest, where the first tract of national forest land in the eastern United States along Curtis Creek was dedicated to his efforts.

Buncombe County

Phone Number
- (828) 298-0358

Website
- nps.gov/blri

Admission Fee
- None

Park Hours
- Sunrise to sundown although Parkway access closes in winter

Directions
- *Blue Ridge Parkway*; Milepost 374.4 on roadside at south end of Tanbark Tunnel.

Ambler built Rattlesnake Lodge in 1904 as a private summer home, all with hand-hewn chestnut logs. After his wife died in 1918 he never returned and sold the 1,300 acres he had acquired here to the Forest Service for $10 an acre. The lodge, which earned its name from a reported 41 rattlesnakes killed on the property in the first three years, burned to the ground in 1926.

The Walks

From the Blue Ridge Parkway the canine hike to Rattlesnake Lodge is a wedge-shaped affair climbing from the roadbed on either side of a cascading stream with a 2,000-foot connector in the lodge site. Each stem trail is about a half-mile long; the southern prong ends at the remains of the tool shed and the northern prong terminates in front of a stone chimney from a caretaker cabin. The white-circle blazed *Mountains -to-Sea Trail* does the connecting. Once at the lodge site there is plenty of nosing around for your dog to do among the ruins including tennis courts and a hillside potato house to the south and a hooded reservoir up the mountain where the trail continues to form a loop with the *Mountains-to-Sea Trail.*

A fallen tree provides a rustic accent to the ruins of the old Rattlesnake Lodge spring house.

Trail Sense: This is one of the Parkway hikes not listed on official descriptions where travelers drive past and wonder, "why are all the cars parked along the road?"

Dog Friendliness
Dogs are welcome on the Blue Ridge Parkway trails.

Traffic
Foot traffic only when you are off the roadway.

Canine Swimming
The springs and streams on the mountainside are not deep enough for a canine plunge but will provide a cooling splash on a hot day.

Trail Time
About one hour with more hiking for your dog along the *Mountains-to-Sea Trail*, which begins to climb sharply not too far north from Rattlesnake Lodge.

33
Old Fort
Picnic Area

The Park

In the 1770s, in violation of a treaty between the British and the Cherokee Nation, settlers began trickling west of the Blue Ridge Mountains. One such family was the Davidson brothers - John, Samuel, William and George - who owned land at the headwaters of the Catawba River. When the North Carolina militia constructed a wooden garrison at the headwaters to protect settlers from Cherokee raids in 1776 it was called Davidson's Fort and was the westernmost outpost in Colonial America. Over the next 100 years the settlement saw a brief gold craze in the mountain streams, was the site of some Civil War maneuverings in the final days of the conflict and eventually morphed into a resort village when the Western North Carolina Railroad pulled into town in 1870. Renamed Old Fort by the State General Assembly, its days as a tourist mecca slowed when its resort - built a little too conveniently to the railroad - burned in 1903. Old Fort still launches visitors into the Blue Ridge Mountains but today it is on foot and bike, not by carriage and train car.

McDowell County

Phone Number
- (828) 652-2144

Website
- fs.usda.gov/nfsnc

Admission Fee
- None

Park Hours
- Sunrise to sunset

Directions
- *Pisgah National Forest*; from I-40 take Exit 72 towards Old Fort. After about a mile, turn left onto Old Highway 70 and continue to the picnic area on the left, opposite Mill Creek Road. If it is closed there is room to park at the gate and take the short walk inside.

Bonus

Two miles down Mill Creek Road opposite the picnic area entrance you will find a small park containing Andrews Geyser. North Carolina has no natural geysers; this is an artificial water spout built in 1912 by George Fisher Baker of New York as a tribute to his friend Colonel Alexander Boyd Andrews. Andrews was a Confederate Army officer in his early twenties and later was president of the Western North Carolina Railroad. Baker used gravity-fed water from a nearby mountain lake to fashion the geyser. There are no trails in the town-owned park but it is a great place for a game of fetch.

The Walks

The star attraction at the Old Fort Picnic Area is a stretch of Old Highway 70 that has been gated and paved over in stretches to do duty as a biking/hiking trail. The old road winds up the mountainside for about 2.5 miles, gaining 900 feet in elevation, to where a tourist observation platform once stood and cars puttered up the Swannanoa Gap to look over the Royal Gorge. Today's *Point Lookout Trail* goes one mile more to its conclusion near Black Mountain where you can chance to still see trains disappearing into mountain tunnels.

Dogs enjoying a romp at Andrews Geyser.

For more traditional canine hiking fare you can pick up *Young's Ridge Trail* at the back of the picnic area to the left of the restrooms. The path picks its way steadily up to a ridge and eventually the top of Kitsuma Peak in 3.5 miles where the payoff is views of surrounding peaks, including Mount Mitchell on a good day, and more panoramic looks at the railroad. Less romantic are winter views of nearby I-40.

Trail Sense: No maps on site. Stay to the left walking on the old roadbed of *Point Lookout Trail*.

Dog Friendliness
Dogs are allowed on the trails and in the picnic area.

Traffic
These are popular trails; expect both wheeled and footed company.

Canine Swimming
Mill Creek is refreshing but not deep.

Trail Time
Each canine hike at Old Fort Picnic Area will require 2-3 hours.

34
Jackson
Park

The Park

With the prodding of Henderson County Commissioner Clyde Jackson and $120,000 in initial funds, groundbreaking ceremonies for this park were held on April 29, 1974. The park offices were established in a farmhouse on the property designed by Hendersonville's most eminent architect, Erle G. Stillwell. Hannibal, Missouri-born Stillwell had first seen the area in 1905 on a visit to his sister's summer home. He designed his first buildings in Hendersonville in 1913 and transformed the town streetscape, including the creation of City Hall in 1928. Today Jackson Park encompasses 212 acres and is the largest county-owned park in Western North Carolina. It is an active recreation park with basketball courts, tennis courts, softballs fields, and soccer fields. The park's dominant natural feature is Mud Creek that drains most of the precipitation that falls in Hendersonville and eventually deposits it in the Gulf of Mexico.

Henderson County

Phone Number
- (828) 697-4884

Website
- hendersoncountync.org/recreation/jacksonpark.html

Admission Fee
- None

Park Hours
- Sunrise to sunset

Directions
- *Hendersonville*; at 801 Glover Street. From I-26 take Exit 49B onto NC 64. Past the fast food jungle get into the left lane and prepare to turn left at the brown "Jackson Park" sign onto Harris Street. When Harris Street ends at 4th Avenue, turn left into the park.

The Walks

The *Jackson Park Nature Trail* trips through forest swamps and oak-hickory climax forests and open meadows and piney hillsides that will run your dog away from the action on the ballfields. Further explorations can be taken on dirt side trails that poke into crevasses in the wetlands. A paved ribbon called the *Oklawaha Greenway* also dogs Mud Creek for two miles through greenspace to Patton Park. Oklawaha is a Cherokee word translating roughly to "slowly moving muddy waters."

But for all the tranquility Jackson Park, a designated Significant Natural Heritage Area by the State of North Carolina, dishes out, the gem for dog owners here is the dog park. The large open space, fenced in by chain link and Mud Creek and its tributaries, is user-operated in agreement with the park. So there are no signs and no list of rules. To find the dog park from the park office, turn right out of the parking lot and make your first left down the dirt road after the first stream crossing. For water-loving dogs, avoid the mucky creek behind the tent pavilion and go instead across the park to Mud Creek - the water under the railroad trestle is reliably deep enough for dog-paddling.

Trail Sense: Signs lead the way around Jackson Park.

Dog Friendliness
Dogs are welcome, and frequent visitors, to Jackson Park.

Traffic
The Oklawaha Greenway is a multi-use trail.

Canine Swimming
Mud Creek can host canine aquatics at several spots along its length and the waters get frisky after a storm.

Trail Time
Your dog can spend an hour or more on these trails.

35
Craven
Gap

The Park

Sixteen Presidents at some point in their lives visited Asheville, beginning with Rutherford B. Hayes in 1882. Most stayed in the Grove Park Inn, like Barack and Michelle Obama did during a 2010 vacation. But Obama, the ninth Chief Executive to visit the Land of the Sky while in office, was the first to visit the Blue Ridge Parkway or step out for a hike. The place the first couple selected for their adventure on the *Mountains-to-Sea Trail* was the stretch between Craven Gap and Bull Gap.

Buncombe County

Phone Number
- (828) 298-0358

Website
- nps.gov/blri

Admission Fee
- None

Park Hours
- Sunrise to sundown although Parkway access closes in winter

Directions
- *Blue Ridge Parkway*, Milepost 377.4.

"Any man who does not like dogs and want them about does not deserve to be in the White House," President Calvin Coolidge said. Coolidge himself had at least 12 dogs. Subsequent office holders have taken the 29th American President's words to heart - every single one has shared the Oval Office with a canine friend. But the Obamas did not bring First Dog Bo to the Blue Ridge Parkway - don't make the same mistake when you hike in the Presidential footsteps.

The Walks

From Craven Gap north (the Obama's route) the *Mountains-to-Sea Trail* is as level as you will find a mountain trail but there is rock scrambling aplenty to keep your dog entertained. The rock formations, including a small cave, are a highlight of this canine ramble, as are the valley views. The distance to Ox Creek Road is 1.8 miles; the next leg north leads to Rattlesnake Lodge (page 80). South of Craven Gap the trail drops beneath the Parkway for more woods walking with your dog and glimpses into the valley below.

Trail Sense: Craven Gap is not an official Blue Ridge Parkway stop; short feeder trails from the parking area in the Gap lead to the white-circle blazed *Mountains-to-Sea Trail*.

Dog Friendliness
Dogs are welcome on the Blue Ridge Parkway trails.

Traffic
Foot traffic only.

Canine Swimming
None.

Trail Time
The "Obama Hike" will require a leisurely 90 minutes to two hours to complete out-and-back without a Secret Service car shuttle.

36
Big East Fork Trailhead
Transylvania County
Pisgah National Forest; US 276, four miles north of the Blue Ridge Parkway.

This is a way to penetrate the Shining Rock Wilderness Area from beneath the Blue Ridge Parkway. Many canine hikers start down the 3.4-mile *Shining Creek Trail* at the parking lot and follow the lively green waters until some indeterminate turn-around point is reached. You can easily get over an hour of superb canine hiking this way. But the true hike here is a bruising seven-mile loop with the *Old Butt Knob Trail* that crosses several knobs on Chestnut Ridge. Gnarly laurel thickets are a prominent feature of the hiking here, both down by the creek and on the ominously named Dog Loser Knob where you can picture a dog wandering 100 yards off the trail and never being able to find his way back through the branches. The two trails merge at Shining Rock Gap along with the *Art Loeb* and *Investor Gap Trails* and there is minimal signage in wilderness areas such as this so make certain you have your wayfinding gear with you. There are plenty of canine swimming pools in Shining Creek but the cascades are powerful as well so take care. Back at the trailhead your dog will have earned his post-hike treat with pride after this loop.

37
North Mills Recreation Area
Henderson County
Pisgah National Forest; east of Mills River from NC 280, turn north at the sign and travel five miles to the recreation area (paved).

The *North Mills Trail* runs north from the camping area up to Trace Ridge. It is easy trotting for your dog along - and through the river (there are no bridges) with lots of open areas that make this canine hike a best bet for a sunny day. The *Trace Ridge Trail* is heavily eroded on its descent to the river but does not last long. Alternatively you can drive up to Trace Road and access the bulk of the trail system there. The overlooked *Bear Branch Trail* (on the east side of FS 5000 at its intersection with Hendersonville Reservoir Road) is a winner for your dog here. It is a modest climb for a mile through an inviting mixed woodland and you can use the adjoining gated *Seinard Mountain Road* to come back down.

38
Black Mountain Recreation Area

Yancey County

Pisgah National Forest; frm NC 80 north of the Blue Ridge Parkway turn left on South Toe River Road (NFSR 472) to campground (partly gravel).

Black Mountain is your dog's base camp for assaults on Mount Mitchell and Green Knob but it is not all mountaineering here. Less ambitious canine hikers can enjoy the *Devil's Den Nature Trail* that spins away from the amphitheatrer for a half-hour journey through tall hardwoods and some of the best boulders you will see on an Asheville-area trail. The yellow-blazed *Briar Bottom Bicycle Trail* tracks the South Toe River under dark hemlock trees before looping back in 1.2 miles. For waterfall hunters a short trail by the group campground gate leads to Setrock Creek Falls where water zigzags over a multi-layered rock cliff. Back near the turn-off on NC80 (on FR 5520 off FR 20) for the recreation area an easy hike of 3/4 miles on a gated forest road leads to Roaring Fork Falls where water sluices 100 feet down a rock channel into an inviting plunge pool ringed by granite boulders.

39
Sandy Mush Gamelands

Buncombe County

Leicester; from NC 63 take Alexander Road for about three miles to Tipton Hill Road and turn left. At the end in two miles turn left on unsigned Cedar Hill Road and continue to end (last half-mile gravel).

The Sandy Mush Gamelands are managed by the North Carolina Wildlife Resources Commission for hunting, mostly grouse. Hunt days are Monday, Wednesday and Saturday so if you don't want to familiarize yourself with hunting season schedules come on another day. There are orange-gated access points scattered around the 2,679 acres but the best canine hiking starts at the lot at the end of Cedar Hill Road. The old farm road begins stony but turns to paw-friendly grass as it traverses a low ridge with long valley and mountain views. After 15 minutes a trail diverges to the right that fights its way through a hemlock forest - some trees up and some trees down. Your dog will enjoy the obstacle course on the 15-minute descent to the French Broad River where he can cross the railroad tracks and get a swim in the muddy water on a hot day. The main trail continues aways further until it ends of a clover-choked knob. No trails are marked in Sandy Mush so come with a mind for exploring with your dog.

40
French Broad River Park
Buncombe County
Asheville; take Exit 1C of I-240 onto Amboy Road to the park.

Public recreation first came to the banks of the French Broad River in Asheville in 1904 when the Asheville Electric Company built Riverside Park and transported folks out on their trolleys to enjoy the carousel and walking paths. Movies were shown on the banks of the river that could only be viewed by boat. Riverside Park was crippled by a fire in 1915 and completely destroyed by flooding a year later.

In the 1990s development began again with French Broad River Park which won a Heritage Park Award as one of the 10 best parks in America funded with a land and water conservation fund grant. The *French Broad River Greenway* links French Broad River Park and Carrier Park with an hour of canine hiking along a paved, level path tracing the world's third-oldest river (only the Nile River in Africa and the New River in West Virginia are older than the French Broad). Anchoring the corridor in French Broad River Park is a two-section dog park - behind the dog park is your dog's best access from the high banks for a swim.

41
Florence Nature Preserve
Henderson County
Gerton; south of town on US 74.

Tom and Glenna Florence donated these 600 acres on the slopes of Little Pisgah Mountain to the nonprofit Carolina Mountain Land Conservancy and built the trails. There is a climb of thirty minutes from Route 74 to reach the Preserve lands which loop down along a heavily vegetated stream and up to a mountain meadow. The trails are marked and a map can be found but it is still best to come with a mind for exploring in this attractive woodland. Along the way your dog will bump into cascading streams and old cabins.

42
Big Ivy Recreation Area

Buncombe County

Barnardsville; from I-26 take Exit 15 onto NC 197. In Barnardsville turn right on Dillingham Road to National Forest in 6 miles. The road becomes FR 74 and is gravel from that point.

Big Ivy is the name locals have for the mountain laurel shrub. Long abandoned logging roads have been converted into trails in this remote part of Pisgah National Forest. Most are only a mile or two but are universally steep and demanding. The trails typically depart from the ten-miles or so of FR 74, including the star walk at Big Ivy - and the only easy one, a half-mile walk to 70-foot Douglas Falls set in the vestiges of a virgin hemlock forest among scattered battleship-sized boulders. Douglas Falls itself tumbles over one such rock and your dog can scramble up behind it.

**There are so many boulders around
Douglas Falls that the trees
don't have anywhere to grow.**

43
Azalea Park

Buncombe County

Asheville, take Exit 7 off I-240 onto Tunnel Road (US 70 East). Turn right at Swannanoa Road, NC 81, and Left on Azalea Road to the park.

This Asheville greenspace, while primarily a paradise for soccer players, nonetheless serves up a smorgasbord of delights for your dog in small doses. Beyond the fields, short, rutted jeep trails lead to the shallow Swannanoa River that flows in a series of low dams and pools for some superb doggie paddling. For a little cardio there is a gated road opposite that open field which leads up a wooded hillside. And for some socializing there is a fenced-in dog park a little further down Azalea Road.

How To Pet A Dog
Tickling tummies slowly and gently works wonders.
Never use a rubbing motion; this makes dogs bad-tempered.
A gentle tickle with the tips of the fingers is all that is necessary
to induce calm in a dog. I hate strangers who go up to dogs with their
hands held to the dog's nose, usually palm towards themselves.
How does the dog know that the hand doesn't hold something horrid?
The palm should always be shown to the dog and go straight
down to between the dog's front legs and tickle gently with
a soothing voice to accompany the action.
Very often the dog raises its back leg in a scratching movement,
it gets so much pleasure from this.
-Barbara Woodhouse

And because sometimes
the best hikes with
your dog do not take
take place on dirt and
grass...

44.
A Walking Tour of... Downtown Asheville

Begin at Vance Monument in Pack Square...

1. Vance Monument
Pack Square

Born in 1830 in a log cabin in Reems Creek, Zebulon Baird Vance was the son of a farmer and country merchant who grew up to be a lawyer noted for his sharp and earthy wit. Vance entered politcs and became a United States congressman and eloquent supporter of the Union until the very outbreak of the Civil War. Nevertheless, Vance chose loyalty to his home state once hostilities began. In Asheville, he organized the Confederate Rough and Ready Guards; as colonel of the 26th North Carolina Regiment, he gained such fame for his courage that he was elected governor of North Carolina in 1862 and again in 1864. Until his death in 1894 Vance spent most of his time either in the Governor's Mansion or his office in the United States Senate. When he died local benefactor George W. Pack offered to donate $2,000 to help pay for a monument to Vance in front of the Buncombe County Courthouse (then located on the east side of the current Pack Square). By 1898, the obelisk was complete.

WALK OVER TO THE NORTHWEST CORNER OF THE SQUARE AT BROADWAY.

2. Akzona/Biltmore Building
1 North Pack Square

The Akzona/Biltmore Building was created in 1978-80 by internationally renowned architect I. M. Pei, designer of the National Gallery of Art in Washington DC and the Pyramids of the Louvre in Paris. Designed as the headquarters of the Akzona Corporation, this gleaming ultramodern office building replaced an entire block of 1890s buildings along the north side of Pack Square, and was a major component in the late twentieth century revitalization of downtown Asheville.

EXIT PACK SQUARE BY WALKING WEST ON PATTON AVENUE ACROSS BROADWAY.

3. Kress Building
19 Patton Avenue at northwest corner of Lexington Avenue

Samuel Kress founded S.H. Kress & Co. in 1896 and developed five-and-dime stores nationwide. An avid art collector, Kress took pride in creating beautiful buildings and took as much pride in the artistic appearance of his stores as he did in the profits they churned out in the early 1900s. This 1928 storefront/office building features Neoclassic motifs and cream color glazed terra-cotta tile bordered with distinctive blue and orange rosette tiles.

4. Elizabeth Blackwell Bench
Patton Avenue opposite
Church Street

The third of nine children, Elizabeth Blackwell was born in Bristol, England on February 3, 1821. Her parents moved the family to New York City when Elizabeth was 12, and later to Cincinnati where the family's financial fortunes turned for the worse. Elizabeth Blackwell began teaching and came to Asheville and started studying medicine on her own.

Blackwell began seeking a medical school which would accept her. Seventeen rejections later, she sent an application to Geneva Medical College (now Hobart and William Smith Colleges) who believed Blackwell's application to be a joke. In the spirit of good humor, the faculty played along by voting "yes" when her application was presented for vote. So Elizabeth Blackwell became the first woman in America ever to attend medical school. She graduated at the top of her class on January 12, 1849.

She was, however, continually thwarted in her attempts to practice medicine in the United States and in 1869, Blackwell returned to London. She established and ran a large practice, and in 1875 helped to found the London School of Medicine for Women.

5. Drhumor Building
48 Patton Street, southwest corner of Church Street

The Drhumor Building was constructed in 1895 by William J. Cocke, an attorney who studied at the University of North Carolina and at Harvard University. The building was named for the ancestral Irish island of Cocke's Scots-Irish grandfather and rests on the land where Cocke's childhood home and birthplace once stood.

The oldest standing commercial building in downtown Asheville is, appopriately, the work of Asheville's most prominent early architect Allen L. Melton. Many of the important buildings he designed in a life-long career in Asheville have been lost

and this grand Romanesque Revival corner structure remains as his best known work. Biltmore Estate stone carver Frederic Miles was called in to provide the limestone frieze above the first floor exterior. Since 1996 the ornate corner building has housed law offices.

TURN LEFT ON CHURCH STREET.

6. Asheville Federal Savings and Loan Association
11 Church Street

This is the fourth stop on Church Street for the bank that took its first deposits across the street at #12 in 1936. During the early 1960s, the property at 11 Church Street was purchased from First Union National Bank and turned in to current headquarters.

7. Central United Methodist Church
27 Church Street

The congregation began fundraisng for a new church in 1899 and raised enough to hire Reuben Harrison Hunt, one of the late 19th century's most prolific ecclesiastical architects. His powerful Romanesque Revival design with Gothic Revival detailing, rendered in limestone, boasts two pinnacle towers and a five-bay loggia. The first service was held on November 5, 1905.

8. First Presbyterian Church
40 Church Street

The First Presbyterian Church is one of the oldest church buildings in the city. The Gothic Revival church was constructed in 1884 with numerous later additions. The brick nave and tower have deep corbelled cornices and hood-molded windows with blind arcading at the eaves.

9. Trinity Episcopal Church
60 Church Street

The Trinity Episcopal Church was designed by Bertram Goodhue in 1912 in the Tudor Gothic Revival style. The red brick exterior is trimmed with granite and the corner tower is topped with a gabled belfry. Inside, the sanctuary features a fine hammer-beamed ceiling.

RETURN TO PATTON AVENUE AND TURN LEFT.

10. S&W Building
56 Patton Avenue

Frank O. Sherrill and Fred R. Webber, two Western North Carolina natives and former World War I mess sergeants, got their start running the restaurant in Ivey's Department Store in Charlotte. The got the idea of serving food cafeteria style and left to work in cafeterias in Florida and California. When Sherrill and Webber returned to North Carolina they served up the first cafeteria-style food in the state in their S&W Cafeterias.

Asheville's first S&W Cafeteria was located across the street from the Grand Opera House. In 1929, the restaurant moved to Patton Avenue and showcased architect Douglas Ellington's style of combining early Italian Renaissance forms with Art Deco detailing. The exuberant Art Deco masterpiece includes colorful repeating geometric designs of cream, green, blue, black and gilt glazed tiles.

11. Public Service Building
89 Patton Avenue

Erected in 1929, just before the stock market nosedived, and executed with a beautifully ornate polychrome terra-cotta exterior and gargoyles at the roofline, the Public Service Building is a fine example of neo-Spanish Romanesque design.

TURN RIGHT ON OTIS STREET.

12. US Post Office and Courthouse
11 Otis Street

The former United States Post Office and Courthouse, a fine Depression-era Federal Building with Art Deco detailing was designed by James A. Wetmore of the Federal Architect's Office and built in 1929-30. This massive presentation of Asheville architecture is sheathed in limestone with low relief panels and metal doors. Inside, the classic lobby has a stenciled ceiling.

TURN RIGHT ON WALL STREET.

13. Wall Street

Wall Street remembers the retaining wall that held up a 70-foot high hill in the early days of Asheville.

14. Miles Building
14-20 Haywood Street

In 1901, the 20-year-old Asheville Club decided to build itself an impressive new home on land owned by one of its members, Tench Francis Coxe, at the corner of Haywood Street and "Government Street" (now College Street) and a stately three-story mansion with flanking columns was dutifully erected. The Asheville Club's membership rolls were filled with the prominent names that still adorn buildings and streets all over town – Grove, Carrier, Coxe, Rankin, Sluder, Hilliard, Rumbough.

It was Herbert Delahaye Miles who transformed the building from a dignified but rather conventional structure into a unique artifact of Asheville's architectural heyday, the Roaring '20s. He was a vice president of Armour & Co. meatpackers in Chicago when his wife contracted tuberculosis. The doctors prescribed a standard treatment: move to the famously pure air of either Arizona or Asheville. Miles chose Asheville.

In order to have an occupation here, Miles bought the building in 1919 from the Coxe estate, which owned the whole block fronting College Street, and set about converting his new property into office space by adding a striking Italianate exterior on the lower floors that turned the building into a dark red-brick devil's food cake layered with white terra-cotta frosting. If you go in the Wall Street entrance the wide hallways designed for the 1901 Asheville Club still remain.

15. Flatiron Building
10-20 Battery Park Avenue

One of the most famous buildings on the Asheville streetscape, the Flatiron Building was designed by Albert C. Wirth and constructed in 1925-26. Wirth was a Buffalo native who came to North Carolina in 1916 and practiced for 15 years beofre returning to New York. here he delivered an elegant Beaux Arts flavored 8-story office building faced with limestone. The term "Flatiron" refers to its triangular wedge shape that was created to fit the irregular lot. Indeed, its eastern side is just barely wide enough to accommodate an entry door.

TURN LEFT ON
BATTERY PARK AVENUE.

16. Grove Arcade
Battery Park Avenue to
Battle Square

Often acclaimed as one of downtown Asheville's most beautiful buildings, the Grove Arcade covers an entire city block. Commissioned by Edwin Wiley Grove and designed by Charles Newton Parker it was built in 1926-29 as one of America's last classic indoor shopping arcades (before the modern era of malls). Sheathed in ivory hued terra-cotta tile, this Neo-Gothic emporium is softened and embellished with rich detailing around the roof line and windows. The most dramatic entrance is from the north side, along Battle Square, guarded by a pair of winged lion sculptures.

Inside, the grand central corridor of this elegant structure is a striking two-story arcade ornately decorated with medieval-style grotesques, shields tucked into Roman-style niches, Gothic-flavored pointed arches and spiraling wrought-iron staircases. Overhead, a peaked glass ceiling fills the space with diffused sunlight. As grand as Parker's building is, it was originally envisioned as an even grander edifice with the addition of a central 14-story office tower which was never built.

TURN RIGHT ON
O'HENRY AVENUE.

17. Citizen-Times Building
14 O'Henry Avenue

At the time the building opened under publisher/owner Charles Webb in 1939, the Art Moderne styled headquarters was hailed as one of the most progressive structures of its kind in the United States and housed the Asheville Citizen, the Asheville Times and WWNC radio station.

18. Battery Park Hotel
1 Battle Square between O'Henry and Page avenues

William L. Stoddart was famous in the 1920s for designing big-city high-rise hotels in towns of modest size. Edwin Wiley Grove financed the Battery Park Hotel in 1923-24 as the first affordable commercial hotel in Asheville built for businessmen and tourists. It replaced the ornate Queen Anne style Battery Park Hotel owned by entrepreneur and railroad mogul Frank Coxe, which was built in 1886. George Vanderbilt stayed there and Theodore Roosevelt and most of the famous visitors who found their way to Asheville at the turn of the 20th century. The original Battery Park Hotel also stood some eighty feet above the current one, as it was placed on a hill that Grove later removed in its entirety to make room for more construction in the downtown area. Stoddart's T-plan Neo-Georgian hotel is reinforced concrete faced in red brick with limestone and terracotta details. Today the Battery park survives as an apartment complex.

TURN LEFT ON PAGE AVENUE.

19. Basilica of St. Lawrence
97 Haywood Street

This impressive Spanish Baroque Revival Roman Catholic Church is the masterpiece created by internationally renowned Spanish architect/engineer Rafael Guastavino with the help of architect Richard Sharp Smith from 1905-09. Guastavino worked on the Biltmore Estate when he first came to Asheville, but soon decided that the town required a larger Catholic Church. He enlisted the support of his friend Smith, and they planned this spacious and ornate building. The magnificent exterior of red brick stands atop a stone foundation and is built entirely without wood or steel, relying solely on masonry and tile for the floors, ceiling and pillars. The dome is believed to be the largest freestanding elliptical dome in North America. You can enter a side door that opens into the church, where the ornate interior is adorned with exceptional tile work and religious art.

20. Basilica of St. Lawrence Rectory
Haywood Street

The rectory for the Basilica of St. Lawrence was built next door in 1929.

TURN RIGHT ON
HAYWOOD STREET.

21. Asheville Civic Center
87 Haywood Street

The Asheville Civic Center is a regional destination for outstanding entertainment, trade shows and events. The bronze figures out front celebrate musical heritage of Appalachia.

22. George Vanderbilt Hotel
75 Haywood Street

Hotel specialist William Stoddard was back at work in 1924 with this nine-story structure. The George Vanderbilt Hotel opened with great fanfare and is now used as a seniors' residence known as Vanderbilt Apartments.

23. Castanea Building
57-65 Haywood Street

This historic building has anchored the center of Haywood Street since 1921 when it housed among other tenants, the YWCA.

24. Asheville Hotel
northeast corner of Haywood and Walnut streets

The Asheville Hotel Building began life in 1915 as Asheville Elks Lodge #608 although today it is neither. Designed by the prolific partnership of Albert Heath Carrier and Richard Sharp Smith, the building was one of the most modern Elks lodge in the southern states. Carrier and Smith designed some 700 buildings in Western Carolina in a variety of styles. Inside this building, "no expense was spared to make it modern in every detail." In 1931, the building was remodeled and renamed the Asheville Hotel; in 1957 the building was converted into a downtown department store and today houses shops, an eatery and condos.

25. Woolworth Company Store
25 Haywood Street

This store for the iconic five-and-dime chain was designed by Henry I. Gaines in the late Art Deco minimalist style and built in 1939. Completely renovated and restored in 2001, Woolworth's was returned to its original splendor, including the decorations above the exterior windows and the red sign over the entrance. Inside the grand staircase and terrazzo floors are original, and a 50's style soda fountain has been rebuilt in its original location. It now showcases the works of local artists.

RETURN TO WALNUT STREET AND TURN RIGHT. TURN LEFT ON BROADWAY STREET.

26. Masonic Temple
80 Broadway Street

The Ancient Free and Accepted Mason is a fraternal order with a worldwide membership, thought to have arisen from practicing stone masons and cathedral builders in the early Middle Ages. The lodge, first formed in early 18th-century England, is the basic organizational unit. Philadelphia Lodge, formed in 1730, is the oldest Masonic lodge in the United States. The Mount Hermon Masonic Lodge of Asheville was chartered on December 13, 1848, with 107 members, and counted numerous civic and political leaders among them. The lodge had no formal meeting place for more than 50 years until 1909, when the 500 members passed a resolution to acquire a site for the Masonic Temple.

The local architectural firm of Smith & Carrier designed all the fraternal organizations in Asheville, including the Elks Home, Eagles Home and the Asheville Club. The Masonic Temple, designed in 1913 and occupied in 1915, is the only fraternal building that retains its original use. Fronting on Broadway, the striking edifice features robust brickwork and is dominated by a tall portico of paired Ionic columns and a three-story, blind arched window on its Woodfin Street side.

TURN RIGHT ON WOODFIN STREET AND RIGHT AGAIN ON NORTH MARKET STREET.

27. Thomas Wolfe House
152 North Market Street

The sprawling frame Queen Anne-influenced house was originally only six or seven rooms with a front and rear porch when prosperous Asheville banker Erwin E. Sluder constructed it in 1883. By 1889 massive additions had more than doubled the size of the original house, but the architecture changed little over the next 27 years.

In Look Homeward, Angel Thomas Wolfe accurately remembered the house he moved to in 1906 as a "big cheaply constructed frame house of 18 or 20 drafty, high-ceilinged rooms." Wolfe lived here until 1916, when he entered the University of North Carolina. In 1916 Wolfe's mother, Julia Westall Wolfe, enlarged and modernized the house, adding electricity, additional indoor plumbing, and 11 rooms. Julia did not operate the boardinghouse out of any financial necessity. Thomas Wolfe's father, W. O. Wolfe, could well afford to support the family with the earnings of the tombstone shop he owned and operated on Asheville's city square. But Julia, a former teacher, had an obsession for the real estate market and used her profits to buy more property. Descendants remembered Julia, a shrewd and uncompromising businesswoman, as a "driver of hard bargains."

TURN LEFT ON COLLEGE STREET TO COURT PLAZA.

28. Buncombe County Court House
60 Court Square

Originally this building was designed to be a matching Art Deco structure by Douglas D. Ellington to City Hall next door, but the politics of the day intervened when the county commissioners dissented and commissioned an intentionally more conservative building. This conventional 17-floor Neoclassical steel frame structure with a brick and limestone surface was designed by Milburn and Heister of Washington DC and built from 1927-28. The courthouse's distinctive setbacks, window groupings and ornamentation were considered opulent in a time when many public buildings were much more conservative. Take time to walk inside to admire the lobby with its impressive mosaic floor, sweeping marble staircase and ornate plasterwork on the coffered ceiling.

29. Asheville City Building
70 Court Square

The Asheville City Building is a colorful, massive and eclectic Art Deco masterpiece. Douglas D. Ellington, an architect who came to Asheville in the mid-1920s, designed the eight-story building, which was completed in 1928. Ellington stated that the design was "an evolution of the desire that the contours of the building should reflect the mountain background."

Ellington chose building materials that presented a "transition in color paralleling the natural clay-pink shades of the local Asheville soil." The unusual octagonal roof is covered with bands of elongated triangular terra cotta red tiles. Between the two levels of the roof are angular pink Georgia marble piers between which are precise vertical rows of ornamental green and gold feather motifs.

WALK BACK TOWARDS PACK SQUARE AND TURN LEFT ON SPRUCE STREET.

30. Mt. Zion Missionary Baptist Church
47 Eagle Street at southeast corner of Spruce Street

The congregation was founded in the 1890s and this, the third church building, dates to 1919.

TURN RIGHT ON EAGLE STREET.

31. Young Men's Institute
39 South Market Street at southeast corner of Eagle Street

In 1893 George Vanderbilt had this English Tudor Cottage-style rec center built for men who worked on Biltmore. The building was utilized as a social and educational center by the African American community in the segregated South. The structure is listed on the National Register of Historic Places.

TURN RIGHT ON MARKET STREET AND TURN LEFT ONTO PACK SQUARE.

32. Jackson Building
22 South Pack Square

The tall slender building on the corner was the first skyscraper in Western North Carolina, erected in 1923-24. Ronald Greene draped his Neo-Gothic confection in terra cotta and crowned it with stone gargoyles. In its early days, one of the building's most unusual uses was as a "clean-air lookout." Many of Asheville's buildings were heated with coal, and every morning the city inspector stood at the top of the Jackson Building to watch for excessive smoke as building furnaces started up. If heavy smoke persisted for more than 5 minutes a citation to clean the furnace was issued.

33. Westall Building
20 South Pack Square

Ronald Greene next went to work on this 8-story office tower in 1925, tapping the Spanish-Romanesque style for the Westall Building. The Westall was not large enough for its own elevator so the two buildings have the same elevator system.

34. Commerce Building
18 South Pack Square

This Neoclassical building in the center of the square dates to 1904.

35. Legal Building
10-14 South Pack Square

Albert Heath Carrier and Richard Sharp Smith raised one of the first buildings in town with reinforced concrete for this imposing 5-story Renaissance Revival building in 1909. It was the home of the Central Bank and Trust Company which collapsed in 1930.

36. Asheville Art Museum
2 South Pack Square

The original Renaissance Revival Pack Memorial Library was designed by Edward L. Tilton of New York. Faced with white Georgian marble and featuring a dramatic two story arched entry with matching banks of arched windows this striking building was completed in 1926. The library and the adjoining theater were renovated into an Education-Arts-Science center in a $15 million project. Pack Place opened in 1992.

YOU HAVE NOW RETURNED TO YOUR STARTING POINT.

45.
A Walking Tour of...
Historic Montford

Begin at Montford Park...

1. Montford Park
between Montford and Cumberland avenues on Panola Street/Montford Park Place

George Willis Pack was born on a upstate New York farm in 1831 and followed his family to the northlands of Michigan while in his twenties. In Port Huron he and his father established one of the first sawmills, called Pack's Mills, in the Black River area. From there Pack continued to amass timberlands and lumber companies before taking his sizable fortune to Cleveland in the 1870s when that Great Lakes city ranked only behind the great Eastern seacoast cities in prominence. He soon became one of the leading citizens of Cleveland. In 1884 Pack and his family relocated to Asheville for health reasons. Pack's generosity to his adopted hometown is legendary with influences in virtually every aspect of Asheville life. He is best known for giving the land that is Pack Square in the heart of Asheville but he also donated four acres of land here for Montford Park. The park was said to once serve up the most beautiful spring floral display in Asheville but today is more of a recreational space.

WALK DOWNHILL THROUGH THE PARK OVER TO CUMBERLAND AVENUE. ACROSS THE STREET, ON THE NORTHEAST CORNER OF CUMBERLAND CIRCLE, IS...

2. The Frances
333 Cumberland Avenue

No grand architectural pedigree here, just a bit of Merrye Olde England rendered in brick and cast concrete to kick off the walking tour.

CROSS OVER ONTO CUMBERLAND CIRCLE AND BEGIN WALKING UP.

3. Applewood Manor Inn
62 Cumberland Circle

When the lots for this small enclave of Montford went up for sale in the early 1900s the deed restriction required that at least $2,500 be spent to build. That was no problem for John Adams Perry who lavished $8,000 on his one-and-a-half acre plot, hiring William Henry Lord to design a timeless Colonial Revival residence, dressed in cedar shake siding around a pedimented central hall entrance. The house was finished in 1912. Perry was a member of one of America's most distinguished Naval families - his uncles were Commodore Oliver Hazard Perry who became the American hero of the War of 1812 when he scuttled the British fleet in the Battle of Lake Erie and Commodore Matthew Galbraith Perry who opened Japan for trade with the West in 1853. John Perry's father was an Army officer when he was born in Fort Leavenworh in Kansas in 1859; the son went on to become an Army captain as well. Perry lived here until he died in 1939.

4. Abbington Green
Bed & Breakfast Inn
46 & 48 Cumberland Circle

Richard Sharp Smith was born in Yorkshire, England in 1852 and picked up his architecture training on the job. He sailed to America in 1882 and landed in the office of Richard Morris Hunt. In 1889 he received the plum assignment to come to Asheville as Hunt's supervising architect of the Biltmore House. When the 250-room chateau was completed Smith stayed in town and hung out his own shingle. He found himself quickly immersed in a busy practice, including designing more than two dozen buildings in Biltmore Village. Smith also won scores of commissions in Montford and more than any other architect was responsible for shaping the appearance of the Asheville streetscape of the early 1900s. This substantial Colonial Revival-flavored home spanned two Cumberland Circle building lots and was completed in 1908 for David Latorette Jackson, who owned the Euneeda Bakery and Dairy. Wythe Peyton, one of the state's first highway engineers, purchased the house in 1921.

CONTINUE TO THE INTERSECTION WITH CUMBERLAND AVENUE AND SOCO STREET. ACROSS THE STREET, IN THE ELBOW OF CUMBERLAND AND SOCO, IS...

5. At Cumberland Falls Bed & Breakfast Inn 254 Cumberland Avenue

This National Register of Historic Places property dates to the turn of the 20th century and was constructed with maintenance-intensive shingles over weatherboards.

IMMEDIATELY ON YOUR LEFT IS...

6. Whiteford G. Smith House 249 Cumberland Avenue

Whiteford G. Smith was a Greenwood, South Carolina native who graduated form the Maryland Pharmaceutical College in 1890 when he was 31 years old. He arrived in Asheville a year later and found work with the T.C. Smith Drug Company but was running his own apothecary on Patton Street by 1894. Smith, a veteran of both the Spanish-American War and World War I, built a Queen Anne home at 263 Haywood Street that is now on the National Register of Historic Places before moving here.

TURN LEFT ON
CUMBERLAND AVENUE.

7. Holy Trinity Greek Orthodox Church 227 Cumberland Avenue

Founded in 1922 by a tiny band of Greek immigrants, the congregation likes to remind folks that Greek was the principle language of the civilized world until the Fall of Constantinople in 1453 and is still the tongue of 13 million people worldwide. The current property was acquired in 1958 and the Mediterranean-styled church erected. Since 1986 the popular Greek Festival has been held on the grounds each September.

8. Carolina Bed and Breakfast 177 Cumberland Avenue

Richard Sharp Smith tapped the nascent Arts & Crafts movement for this 2 1/2-story home in 1901. The pebble-dash stucco was a favorite building material of Smith and a hallmark of the English-based country style - look for it around Montford. Smith's client here was Maria Brown but she never lived in the house, marrying and moving out of town instead. Her brother took over the property after living in New Zealand where their father was in the foreign service. After Vance Brown, president of the Asheville Mica Company, died in 1933 the building did duty as a boarding house before being resuscitated as a bed and breakfast.

9. The Cumberland Apartments
141 Cumberland Avenue

These three-story brick apartments are distinguished by a quartet of full-height, fluted Ionic columns, ornamental brickwork and a fanlight over the Federal-style entrance. Its twin, the Colonial, albeit with keystones, is down the street.

10. A Bed of Roses
135 Cumberland Avenue

Oliver Davis Revell was born in the middle of the Civil War in Camden, South Carolina. After the war his widowed mother brought her brood to Asheville to live with family. When his mother died when he was 16, Revell was on his own and taught himself to be a carpenter. Described as frugal to a fault, Revell had purchased a lot and constructed a small house to rent out by the time he was 19. By the 1890s he was building homes in the eclectic Queen Anne style around Asheville, of which this property constructed in 1897 stands as his best survivor. It was an investment property for Carolyn Gray, whose husband was a retired Union Army officer. After John Grey died, Revell married his widow. In 1902 the Revells migrated west to the booming Indian Territory, soon to be Oklahoma, where he built four

offices buildings in Muskogee as the town's leading developer.

11. Redwood House
90 Cumberland Avenue

This splendidly maintained Colonial Revival with pitched gable roofs was once the home of Henry Redwood. Redwood was born in Baltimore but ran away to enlist in the Confederate Army when he was 16. During the war he met Edward Dilworth Latta, who would one day be known as the "Pioneer Builder of Charlotte." The two worked together in a clothing store in New York City after the war. In the 1870s Latta and Redwood parted, each going into business for himself in Charlotte and Asheville, respectively. Redwood eventually became vice-president of the American National Bank; his wife held a similar position with the United Daughters of the Confederacy.

TURN LEFT AND WALK DOWN ELIZABETH STREET ACROSS FROM THE REDWOOD HOUSE. TURN RIGHT ON ELIZABETH PLACE.

12. Rankin-Bearden House
32 Elizabeth Place

Built between 1846 and 1848, this is the oldest surviving wood-frame house in Asheville. William Dinwiddie Rankin was born in 1804 in Tennessee, less than a decade after the state was admitted to the Union. He operated a successful frontier commissary in Newport, just across the state line, until the 1840s when his wife Elizabeth was smitten with the tiny mountain town of Asheville during a visit. The Rankins acquired about 75 acres on this wooded hillside and constructed this substantial five-bay, two-story house. William

Rankin transferred his mercantile interests to Asheville and also operated the area's largest tannery on the property. He put in a stint as mayor of the town from and served during the Civil War as a member of the "Silver Greys" - men who were too old to serve but protected the homefront. The house was raided by Yankee troops and during a skirmish on April 3, 1865 took a cannonball in one of its chimneys. In 1879 William Rankin was kicked in the head by a mule and died at the age of 75. The family began selling parcels of land that would become the Town of Montford but remained in the house until 1912. A century later you can still see the Greek Revival form and entranceway with transom and sidelights. The porch and bracketing are Victorian affectations added in the post-Civil War period.

TURN RIGHT ON
STARNES AVENUE.

13. Brexton Boarding House
33 Starnes Avenue

When the railroad in the late 1800s opened access to Asheville's clean mountain air to less well-heeled vacationers, furnished boarding houses began to spring up to accommodate these new middle class tourists. "The Brexton," an architecturally undistinguished form of the breed, opened in the mid-1890s. In 1906, the Sisters of Mercy operated a sanitarium out of the house when St. Joseph's Hospital owned the building. To ease the suffering of their tubercular patients sleeping porches were added to the outside and these can still be seen today behind the modern siding.

CONTINUE TO THE END OF
STARNES AVENUE AND TURN
RIGHT ON CUMBERLAND
AVENUE AND THEN TURN LEFT
ON BEARDEN AVENUE TO ITS
END. ON YOUR LEFT AT
MONTFORD AVENUE IS...

14. Gudger House
89 Montford Avenue

Henry Lamar Gudger, the Asheville postmaster, purchased this property at the gateway to the Montford District in 1890. He constructed a rambling Queen Anne frame house awash with gables and towers which remained in the family until the 1950s. Afterward came a familiar tale of subdivision and decline into disrepair. In 1978 the condemned Gudger House was acquired by the Preservation Society of Asheville and Buncombe County and became one its first success stories.

15. Urban Quad
111-113 Montford Avenue

Here is a modern take on the Arts and Crafts styling that permeates the Montford streetscape. The grouping of four houses form an "urban quad" that stand in the stead of a razed mansion.

16. Montford Arts Center
135 Montford Avenue

The future of American retailing changed forever on September 6, 1916 when Clarence Saunders opened the first Piggly Wiggly food store at the corner of Jefferson Avenue and Main Street in Memphis. Until that time, customers presented their lists at a front counter and clerks went to collect the goods and weigh out ground coffee scooped from large wooden barrels. At Piggly Wiggly, shoppers wandered the aisles and filled their own carts with items they plucked from the shelves. Within five years Saunders had franchised self-service groceries in 40 states, ushering in the age of the supermarket. This brick building was constructed in 1926 as a Piggly Wiggly grocery store. Over the years it has done time as a North Asheville police station and is currently gallery space for local artists and craftsfolk.

17. Morris Lipinsky House
211 Montford Avenue

Before turning left and continuing to tour Montford Avenue, look across the street to the right to see the tell-tale gambrel roof of the Dutch Colonial Revival home of Morris Lipinsky. Like his father before him and his son afterwards, Lipinsky was a downtown Asheville merchant. Starting as an errand boy, Lipinsky worked his way to the presidency of the Bon Marche department stores.

18. The Lion & The Rose Bed & Breakfast
276 Montford Avenue

Elmer Horace Craig was a Special Examiner in the United States Pension Office in Wisconsin when his health broke. Seeking relief he brought his family to Asheville where they moved into this classically-flavored Victorian house in 1896. Craig could only enjoy it a short time, however, before he died at the age of 51 in 1898. His wife Charity, daughter of Jeremiah McLain Rusk, a Civil War general, three-time governor of Wisconsin and the second United States Secretary of Agriculture, managed the household thereafter. She was a President of the Women's Relief Corps whose purpose was to perpetuate the memory of the Grand Army of the Republic. Charles and Ethel Toms bought the house after Charity Craig's death in 1913. The house is centered around a flamboyant gable above a wraparound porch with double Doric supports on stone pedestals.

19. The Black Walnut Bed & Breakfast Inn
288 Montford Avenue

Here is another design from the pen of Richard Sharp Smith, created in 1899 for Ottis Green with elements from the Craftsman and Colonial Revival styles. Green was a graduate of Trinity College before it became Duke University and operated a prosperous hardware concern on Pack Square. He also served as mayor of Asheville in the 1930s. It is said that, after receiving a tip during the Depression, Green led a procession of employees - some with shotguns at the ready - to the Central Bank and Trust Company to take all his money away in a wheelbarrow. The next day the bank failed.

20. The 1900 Inn on Montford
296 Montford Avenue

Here is another Richard Sharp Smith creation. Smith was nimble working across a number of styles and this interpretation of an old English field house was designed for Charles S. Jordan, a physician who had recently returned from serving as a first assistant surgeon in the Spanish-American War.

RETRACE YOUR STEPS TO WANETA STREET AND TURN RIGHT. AS WANETA DISSOLVES INTO PEARSON DRIVE, CONTINUE ON PEARSON.

21. Griffith House
224 Pearson Drive

Charles Newton Parker came to Asheville from Ohio in his teens after the death of his father. The year was 1900. He embraced the outdoor lifestyle and found work as a surveyor and then as a draftsman for the City of Asheville in 1906 when he 21. Parker opened his own shop in 1913 and two years later became one of the first licensed architects in North Carolina, issued license certificate #28. He specialized in English Tudor Revival houses in Asheville's new suburbs and this half-timbered brick house, designed in 1920 for Robert W. Griffith, is a superb example. A few years later Parker won the commission to build a massive indoor shopping center for drug manufacturer Edwin W. Grove and the Grove Arcade became his crowning achievement.

22. Cocke House
230 Pearson Drive

This Dutch Colonial Revival corner house - note the trademark Gambrel roof - was the property of Charles Hartwell Cocke and built in 1924. Cocke was born in Columbus, Mississippi, where his father was the president of Mississippi College for Women, in 1881 and earned a medical degree from Cornell University in 1905. Practicing in Birmingham, Alabama he contracted tuberculosis during which he convalesced in New York's Adirondack Mountains. Afterwards he shunned the city and moved to Asheville in 1911 where he became medical director of Zephyr Hill Sanatorium, a governor for North Carolina of the American College of Physicians and author of numerous papers on tuberculosis and internal medicine.

23. Wright Inn and Carriage House
235 Pearson Drive

Osella and Leva Wright ran a leather goods shop called the Carolina Carriage House on Patton Avenue when they built this picturesque Queen Anne residence in 1899. With its irregular roofline, multiple gables and asymmetrical massing it is an exemplary example of the form. The Victorian showcase is a George Barber design. In 1888 George Franklin Barber, an Illinois architect, relocated to Knoxville, hoping the mountain air would restore his declining health. While in town he mastered the technique of mail order architecture, issuing The Cottage Souvenir No. 2 in 1890 with 59 house plans. Barber's designs have resulted in houses in all 50 states. The Wrights sold the house in 1913 and the same day Leva Wright bought back a portion of the property. She remained here taking in boarders until 1945.

24. Williamson House
301 Pearson Drive

William Henry Lord was a native of upstate New York who migrated to Asheville in the late 1890s and became one of the region's leading architect. In the last years of his life when commissions dried up during the Great Depression Lord and his son, also a prominent architect, produced ornamental ironwork at a forge on Flint Street, supplying prestigious clients throughout the East. Here Lord designed an addition in 1906 for the Dutch Colonial with cedar shakes from 1893. The owner was William B. Williamson who began his career in Asheville peddling furniture and later became a banker.

TURN RIGHT ON SANTEE STREET.
TURN RIGHT ON MONTFORD
AVENUE. TURN LEFT ON
ZILLICOA STREET.

25. Homewood
19 Zillicoa Street

Dr. Robert Sproul Carroll came from Duke University to Asheville in 1904 to open Highland Hospital, based on Carroll's theories of electroshock and insulin-therapy for the treatment of mental illness. In 1927 he constructed this Norman-influenced manor house of uncoursed stone highlighted by a corner turret. The pride of Homewood was the 1,500 square foot piano room where Carroll's second wife, Grace Stewart Potter, a concert pianist, would perform and give lessons. At other times, Bela Bartok, regarded as Hungary's greatest composer, would give private concerts here. Carroll remained the director of Highland Hospital until 1944; four years later "Dr. Carroll's Sanitorium" made the headlines when a kitchen fire killed nine women, including author Zelda Fitzgerald, the wife of F. Scott Fitzgerald, who had been a patient off and on since 1936. Homewood is currently an event and conference center.

26. Hopewell Hall
49 Zillicoa Street

James Edwin Rumbough was the only mayor the Town of Montford ever had, serving from 1892 until its annexation by Asheville in 1905. This splendid hilltop manor house was worthy of a man of such distinction, considered the finest residence in all of Montford, but James Rumbough had little to do in its creation. Rather it was his father-in-law, James Baker, a Philadelphia inventor who

not only paid for the construction of the house as a wedding gift in 1892 but attended to every detail, right down to picking each piece of lumber. It seems the Bakers never built with any lumber that wasn't at least 60 years old. Rumbough, the son of an old stage coach operator and owner of the Mountain Park Hotel in Hot Springs, was an early automobile enthusiast. In 1905 he became the first person to drive a car from Asheville to New York City - a trip that took 14 days. In 1911 Rumbough became the first motorist to drive across the Appalachian Mountains into Tennessee.

RETRACE YOUR STEPS BACK TO
MONTFORD AVENUE AND TURN
LEFT.

27. Powell House
346 Montford Avenue

Bricks were not a trendy building material in Montford but this Colonial Revival mansion from 1908 used the familiar clay blocks. It became the Norburn Hospital in 1928 under the guidance of brothers Russell Lee and Charles Norburn. Despite taking care of over 33,000 bed patients, the hospital struggled to survive through the Depression, when few patients could afford to pay their medical expenses. The hospital was eventually taken over by the Mission Memorial Hospital. After the Highland Hospital was destroyed by fire it relocated here. This is another design of William Henry Lord, drawn up for George S. Powell, a businessman and first president of the Appalachian National Park Association.

YOU HAVE NOW RETURNED TO
THE TOUR STARTING POINT AT
MONTFORD PARK.

Five Worth The Drive...

A
Gorges
State Park

The Park

In 1999 the State of North Carolina purchased 10,000 remote, rugged acres from the Duke Energy Corporation and turned most of it into the only state park west of Asheville. This is a land of frequent rainfall (100 inches a year), powerful rivers and lush vegetation - so much so that the region lays claim to being the only temperate rain forest east of the Olympic peninsula in the Pacific Northwest. The ground at Gorges State Park rises over 2,000 feet in just four miles, helping to create more waterfalls than any other North Carolina state park.

Transylvania County

Phone Number
- (828) 966-9099

Website
- ncparks.gov/Visit/parks/gorg

Admission Fee
- None

Park Hours
- Opens at 8:00 a.m. with seasonal closing times through the year

Directions
- *Sapphire*; from Brevard take US 64 west to Sapphire and turn left on NC 281. The park entrance is .7 miles down on the left.

The Walks

The park is still being developed leaving most of Gorges a very wild place but access is open to its star attraction - the Horsepasture River and Rainbow Falls. The Horsepasture takes its pastoral name from a yawning alluvial plain formed where the Laurel Fork Creek flows into the Toxaway River. By the time the river reaches the gorges here it is a whole other beast. Five named hydrospectaculars are created by the churning waters, highlighted by the 125-foot tumble at Rainbow Falls into a natural amphitheater. The trail to the stage is 1.5 miles and novice canine hikers will want to take it slow, especially near the end where it gets steep and involves a lot of high-stepping for you and jumping for your dog. The falls are actually on national forest property but the only legal access is through the state park. Additional canine hiking continues past and above the falls where Turtleback Falls is a popular swimming and sliding hole - it may look like fun but people do get swept over the falls so keep your dog out of the water. On your way back you can safely let your dog into the Horsepasture River for a swim if the water is low. Until further development there are few hiking options with your dog in Gorges State Park unless your taste runs to long, linear back-country road-trails.

Trail Sense: The trail to Rainbow Falls is blazed in orange, stick to it until the park develops.

Many consider Rainbow Falls the top waterfall to hike to with your dog in Western Carolina.

Dog Friendliness

Dogs are allowed to hike the trails in the state park and into national forest property.

Traffic

With only one main hiking trail in the park's infancy the parking lot can fill up on good weather weekends.

Canine Swimming

There are some superb canine swimming holes in the Horsepasture River accessed by old fishing paths to the water - but be careful.

Trail Time

Between one and two hours to reach Rainbow Falls and Turtleback Falls and return.

B
Grandfather Mountain

The Park

A few ticks short of 6,000 feet, rugged Grandfather Mountain, a north-south mass featuring four named peaks, boasts more exposed rocks and crags than any other mountain in the Southern Appalachians. Toss its isolation, unusual height, alkaline soils, and moist cool climate into an ecological stew and you get 16 different biomes in one compact park. Donald Mac Rae bought development rights for 16,000 acres around Grandfather Mountain in 1885 which his grandson Hugh Morton, a photographer, inherited when he was 31 in 1952. Morton opened the mountain to tourists as a private attraction until his death in 2006 when it became North Carolina's 34th state park.

several counties

Phone Number
- (828) 733-4337

Website
- grandfather.com

Admission Fee
- Yes, but some hiking for free

Park Hours
- 8/9:00 a.m. to 6/7:00 p.m.

Directions
- *Blue Ridge Parkway*; Milepost 300 for hikers; entrance on US 221.

The Walks

Grandfather Mountain boasts 11 trails and your dog is welcome on all of them. Casual canine hikers will want to pay the admission and access the modest-rated park trails, of which the *Black Rock Nature Trail* is the best. This is a rocky, one-mile adventure that alternates woods and open spaces where views of the mountains and Parkway can be purchased with little effort. A popular option is to cobble a 1-1/2 mile circuit around Grandfather Mountain with your dog on several park trails.

The marquee walk here is *Grandfather Trail* that traipses 2.4 rocky miles out to Calloway Peak. The jumbled boulders and cliff faces are conquered with wooden ladders and cables on both the *Grandfather Trail* and the somewhat easier *Underwood Trail* that could defeat your dog and send you back at MacRae Peak but still with plenty of views in your memory bank.

Athletic dogs can hike Grandfather Mountain for free with a 2,000-foot climb from the Blue Ridge Parkway at the Boone Fork Parking Area. Calloway Peak is over three miles away on the *Boone Scout Trail* with more ladders at the top that may or may not thwart your dog's final ascent. The *Cragway Trail* and an old logging road dubbed the *Nuwati Trail* can be used to create a fine canine hiking loop.

Your dog may think twice before crossing Mile High Swinging Bridge.

From the west trailhead on NC 105 the *Profile Trail* passes through seven distinct natural communities in 2.7 miles before linking into the *Calloway Trail*. Note: you can't hike with your dog into the park for free.

Trail Sense: Signs and maps make navigation easy here.

Dog Friendliness
Dogs are allowed everywhere on Grandfather Mountain except the buildings.

Traffic
Foot traffic only off the park roads.

Canine Swimming
Nothing if your dog's hiking day is confined to the crest but some creeks and streams stand ready for splashing if you are coming from the lower elevations.

Trail Time
Plan on a full day of canine hiking at Grandfather Mountain; if you venture along craggy *Grandfather Trail* allow twice your typical hiking time.

C
Joyce Kilmer Memorial Forest

The Park

Alfred Joyce Kilmer was an unlikely candidate to be immortalized with nature. He was born in New Brunswick, New Jersey in 1886. His father, Fred, was Scientific Director for Johnson & Johnson who helped introduce Johnson's Baby Powder in 1893. The younger Kilmer made money writing definitions for Funk and Wagnalls' The Standard Dictionary until the publication of his short, 12-line verse "Trees" in 1913 made him famous.

Kilmer enlisted in the National Guard after the United States declared war on Germany in 1917 and quickly rose to the rank of Sergeant. He sought increasingly hazardous duty and during a scouting mission in the Second Battle of the Marne, he was shot though the head and killed at the age of 31. The combination of one wildly popular poem and a promising life cut short have led to far flung memorials to Joyce Kilmer including many in his native state of New Jersey, parks in New York and Chicago, a fireplace in Minnesota, and this forest.

In 1935 the Forest Service purchased land along the Little Tennessee River from the Gennett Lumber Company that included 3,800 acres of woodlands that had never been logged commercially, one of the largest tracts of virgin timber in the Appalachians. The land was dedicated as a living memorial to Joyce Kilmer, a small sliver of the 526,798-acre Nantahala National Forest.

Graham County

Phone Number
- (828) 479-6431

Website
- fs.usda.gov/nfnc

Admission Fee
- None

Park Hours
- Sunrise to sunset

Directions
- Nantahala National Forest; from Robbinsville take NC 143W. After 12 miles, turn right on Joyce Kilmer Road (SR1134) and go two miles to the parking area on the left.

The Walks

The Kilmer Forest is populated with hemlocks and yellow poplars more than 20 feet in circumference and over 450 years old. The only way to see the giants is on foot, via a two-mile figure eight loop, and your dog is welcome. The largest trees are on the upper loop in the Poplar Grove, past the memorial plaque to Kilmer. On the trail don't spend all your time admiring the biggest trees - there are over 100 species of trees in the pristine forest. Basswoods and Northern Red Oaks are two that have grown to spectacular size here.

The downed trees in the Kilmer Forest are almost as impressive as those standing.

There is additional canine hiking on tap here, including the *Naked Ground Trail* that leaves the *Kilmer Memorial Trail* at the Little Santeelah Creek and follows the stream up the valley for almost six miles. There are multiple stream crossings so expect your dog to get her feet wet.

Trail Sense: Trails in this designated wilderness are maintained to the most primitive standards, with few, if any signs or blazes - just remember the trail is a double loop and keep on past the Joyce Kilmer Memorial.

Dog Friendliness
Dogs can be awed by the biggest sticks they will ever see in the Kilmer Forest.
Traffic
No motorized or mechanical vehicles are allowed off the road.
Canine Swimming
Little Santeelah Creek is ot deep enough for dog paddling but stands ready for a refreshing splash.
Trail Time
At least an hour.

Linville Falls

The Park

Lots of states like to anoint a gorge as their "Grand Canyon" and Linville Gorge is North Carolina's designee. The Cherokees called the gorge Eeseeoh, "a river of many cliffs." In 1766 explorer William Linville led a hunting party along the river in violation of an agreement with the Cherokees not to venture into lands west of the Blue Ridge and he and his son were murdered. By 1777 the Cherokees were vanquished and the river, gorge and falls carried Linville's name into history.

Burke County
Phone Number
- (828) 298-0358
Website
- nps.gov/blri
Admission Fee
- Yes, but some hiking for free
Park Hours
- Sunrise to sundown although Parkway access closes in winter
Directions
- *Blue Ridge Parkway*, Milepost 316.4.

The terrain is so hostile in Linville Gorge that lumber companies couldn't get at the timber, plans to harness the power of the falls for electricity never materialized and summer resort ventures foundered. In 1952 John D. Rockefeller, Jr. donated $92,000 to purchase this land and develop it as one of the crown jewels of the Blue Ridge Parkway.

The Walks

Before your dog is through hiking the several miles of trails at Linville Falls she will see the dramatic hydrospectaculars from every angle. Pushing across the river from the Visitor Center, your first destination is a half-mile spur to the twinned Upper Falls. From there, you'll move up as the water moves down. A sporty climb of almost a mile on *Erwins View Trail* (William Erwin owned most of this land in the early 1800s, which had been doled out as rewards to Revolutionary War veterans) leads to more views of the twisting, churning water that produce the highest volume of any waterfall on the Northern Edge of the Blue Ridge Mountains.

The crowds will disappear on the other side of the Linville River for the rooty and rocky descent to the plunge basin that will keep your dog hopping and panting. The virgin hemlock forest and massive rock walls compete with the river for top scenic billing on this 1.4-mile down-and-back canine hike. Another fork here leads to the Plunge Basin Overlook for your best view of the lower falls. If your dog isn't tuckered out after the climb back out of the

The Upper Falls seem tame but the Linville River is just warming up.

gorge pick up the *Duggers Creek Trail* at the back of the parking lot for an easy stroll to Linville Falls in miniature where a stream tumbles into a little rock channel of its own.

Trail Sense: Everything leaves from the Visitor Center and the layout to the overlook destinations is easy to follow.

Dog Friendliness
Dogs are allowed to hike around Linville Falls.

Traffic
Foot traffic only and less of it on the *Linville Gorge Trail*.

Canine Swimming
The Linville River will look tempting in the plunge basin but the current is swift and people have died in these waters so save splashing for Duggers Creek.

Trail Time
Several hours to view Linville Falls from every photo opportunity.

E
Roan Highlands

The Park

Roan Mountain, dressed in a dark green spruce-fir forest and including the world's largest natural rhododendron garden and the longest stretch of grassy bald in the Appalachian range, has long been considered a treasure of the Blue Ridge Mountains. In 1870 John T. Wilder, a Union Army General famed for his command of the Civil War "Lightning Brigade," bought up 7,000 acres along the top and sides of Roan Mountain. Wilder made his money firing the first blast furnaces in the South after the war and his ironworks manufactured rails for the railroads, including his own narrow gauge railway he built to bring tourists to the top of Roan Mountain. In 1885, Wilder con-

Mitchell County

Phone Number
- (828) 682-6146

Website
- fs.usda.gov/recarea/nfsnc

Admission Fee
- Vehicle parking fee at Roan Mountain; none for the Appalachian Trail lot at Carver's Gap

Park Hours
- Sunrise to sunset

Directions
- *Pisgah National Forest*; from Burnsville take 197N to Red Hill, turn left towards Johnson City, TN (Route 226N). Go 3 miles to Fork Mountain Road #1338; turn right and go to the end of the road. Turn left onto 261N and follow to Carver's Gap and Roan Mountain.

structed the luxurious Cloudland Hotel on the mountaintop, promoted as a health resort that was frequented by captains of American industry and European nobility. The hotel was abandoned by 1910, sunk by exorbitant operating costs, and the mountain's forests were subsequently logged off. When the timber was gone Roan Mountain became part of the Pisgah and Cherokee National Forests in 1941.

The Walks

Roan Mountain is not actually a peak but a high ridge that runs five miles from a low point of 5,500 feet at Carver's Gap to 6,285 feet at Roan High Knob. The knob is accessed from a moderate 1.2-mile canine hike along the *Cloudland Trail*. In mid-June the hundreds of acres of Catawba rhododendrons erupt into a magenta riot, luring thousands of visitors to the mountain-top to travel through the canyons of blooms on a paved trail. The two-mile road from Carver's Gap to the gardens is closed from the end of October through March but you can hike - or ski - in with your dog as the case may be.

As remarkable as Roan Mountain is, your dog will likely prefer the canine hiking on the opposite side of Carver's Gap as the *Appalachian Trail* crosses over three grassy balds in less than two hours of hiking. The third, Grassy Ridge Bald, rises to an elevation of 6,189 feet, making it the second highest grassy bald in the Appalachian Mountains. In fact, this is the only stretch of the *Appalachian Trail* that rises above 6,000 feet between Old Black 150 miles to the south and Mount Washington in New Hampshire, 1,500 miles to the north. The views for your dog, of course, are stunning.

Trail Sense: Study the information board for orientation.

Dog Friendliness
Dogs are welcome to enjoy the views from the Roan Highlands.

Traffic
Foot traffic only.

Canine Swimming
None.

Trail Time
As far as your dog wants to hike across the ridge.

30 Waterfalls To Hike To With Your Dog

Waterfalls are some of the most popular destinations on canine hikes. Before setting out to a Blue Ridge waterfall take heed of the signs that warn you that waterfalls are dangerous - people do get injured and die at waterfalls and not just high ones. Heads do not stand up well to rocks. Be vigilant about letting your dog swim around waterfalls - the currents are often stronger they look. And lastly, hikes to waterfalls often meaning heading downhill and that means the hardest part of the canine hike is the last part, unlike on a mountain climb.

Bird Rock Falls
Location: Pisgah National Forest
Directions: Living Waters Ministry on NC 215
Description: wide cascade over 20-foot drop and then slide
Trail: Easy; 1/2-mile
Swimming?: No

Bridal Veil Falls (page 18)
Location: DuPont State Forest
Directions: Fawn Lake Parking Area off Reasonover Road
Description: Long sliding cascade
Trail: Moderate; 2 miles
Swimming?: No

Cedar Rock Falls (page 24)
Location: Pisgah National Forest
Directions: Pisgah Wildlife Education Center, Cat Gap Loop
Description: boulder-studded, 20-foot cascade
Trail: Moderate; 1 mile
Swimming?: No

Courthouse Falls
Location: Pisgah National Forest
Directions: FR 140 off NC 215
Description: 60-foot horsetail plunge into cove
Trail: Easy; 1/4-mile
Swimming?: Yes, but don't let your dog get close - a whirlpool rapid will trap him against the falls

Cove Creek Falls (page 60)
Location: Pisgah National Forest
Directions: FS 475, Caney Bottom and Cove Creek trails
Description: series of cascades under wide veil
Trail: Moderate; I mile
Swimming?: Yes, in large, shallow plunge pool

Crabtree Falls (page 68)
Location: Blue Ridge Parkway
Directions: Crabtree Falls Recreation Area, Milepost 339.5
Description: 70 foot spreading cascade down rock face
Trail: Moderate; 1 mile
Swimming?: No

Daniel Ridge Falls (page 60)
Location: Pisgah National Forest
Directions: FS 475, Daniel Ridge Trail
Description: water hugs rock face for over 100 feet
Trail: Easy; 1/2-mile
Swimming?: No

Douglas Falls (page 91, page 38)
Location: Pisgah National Forest
Directions: Big Ivy Recreation Area, Douglas Falls Trail
Description: 70-foot plunge
Trail: Easy; 1/2-mile
Swimming?: No

French Broad Falls and Mill Shoals Falls
Location: Pisgah National Forest
Directions: Living Waters Ministry on NC 215
Description: twin 20-foot spills over flat rock ledges
Trail: Easy; 50 yards
Swimming?: Yes, in the plunge pool

Grassy Creek Falls (page 18)
Location: DuPont State Forest
Directions: High Falls Parking Area off Station Road
Description: wide slide across rock face
Trail: Moderate; 1.5 miles
Swimming?: No

Graveyard Fields - Second Falls (page 22)
Location: Blue Ridge Parkway
Directions: Graveyard Fields
Description: tiered cascade
Trail: Easy; 1/4-mile
Swimming?: Yes, in the large plunge pool

Graveyard Fields - Upper Falls (page 22)
Location: Blue Ridge Parkway
Directions: Graveyard Fields, Milepost 418
Description: long,sliding cascade
Trail: Easy; 1.25 miles
Swimming?: No

Graybeard Falls (page 22)
Location: Montreat Trails
Directions: Graybeard Trail
Description: rock-clinging 25-foot cascade
Trail: Moderate; 3 miles
Swimming?: No, sitting in the plunge pool though

Grogan Creek Falls (page 24)
Location: Pisgah National Forest
Directions: Pisgah Wildlife Education Center, Butter Gap Trail
Description: creek-wide cascade
Trail: Easy; 1.5 miles
Swimming?: No

Hickory Nut Falls (page 50)
Location: Chimney Rock State Park
Directions: Hickory Nut Falls Trail
Description: Water falls down massive 404-high rock face
Trail: Easy; 1 mile
Swimming?: A plunge pool for splashing

High Falls (page 18)
Location: DuPont State Forest
Directions: High Falls Parking Area off Staton Road
Description: 100-foot cascade
Trail: Easy; about one mile, trail to base
Swimming?: No

Hooker Falls (page 18)
Location: DuPont State Forest
Directions: Hooker Falls Parking Area off Staton Road
Description: 13-foot, river-wide plunge
Trail: Easy; 1/4-mile
Swimming?: Yes, in the large plunge pool

Linville Falls (page 116)
Location: Blue Ridge Parkway
Directions: Linville Falls, Milepost 316.4
Description: small twin falls and a powerful cataract
Trail: Moderate; 1 mile
Swimming?: No

Looking Glass Falls
Location: Pisgah National Forest
Directions: US 276, north of FS 475
Description: 60-foot plunge is area's best-known
Trail: None; steps don to an observation deck
Swimming?: Yes, but don't ruin anyone's photos

Moore Cove Falls (page 55)
Location: Pisgah National Forest
Directions: US 276, Moore Cove Creek Trail
Description: 50-foot plunge over a rock ledge
Trail: Easy; 3/4-mile
Swimming?: No

Rainbow Falls (page 110)
Location: Gorges State Park
Directions: Orange Trail
Description: 125-foot high-volume drop over rockface
Trail: Hardy; 1.5 miles
Swimming?: No

Roaring Fork Falls (page 89)
Location: Pisgah National Forest
Directions: On FR 20 from FR 5520 and NC 80
Description: 100-foot cascade ribbon
Trail: Easy; 3/4-mile
Swimming?: Yes, in the plunge pool

Setrock Creek Falls
Location: Pisgah National Forest
Directions: Black Mountain Recreation Area
Description: disjointed set of tiered cascades
Trail: Easy; 1/4-mile
Swimming?: Yes, in the large plunge pool

Skinny Dip Falls
Location: Blue Ridge Parkway
Directions: Looking Glass Overlook, Milepost 417
Description: segmented cascade
Trail: Easy; 1/2-mile
Swimming?: Yes, in a deep plunge pool

Slick Rock Falls
Location: Pisgah National Forest
Directions: FS 475B off FS 475 off US 276
Description: 35-foot light volume plunge
Trail: Easy; 100 yards
Swimming?: No

Sliding Rock Falls
Location: Pisgah National Forest
Directions: Sliding Rock Recreation Area
Description: sliding cascades over broad round rock
Trail: Easy; 1/4-mile
Swimming?: Yes, in the large plunge pool

Tom's Creek Falls
Location: Pisgah National Forest
Directions: Huskins Branch Road off US 221
Description: 100-foot vertical cascade
Trail: Easy; 1/2-mile
Swimming?: No

Triple Falls (page 18)
Location: DuPont State Forest
Directions: Hooker Falls Parking Area off Staton Road
Description: Triple set of three cascades
Trail: Easy; a half-mile to viewing area, trail to middle
Swimming?: No

Twin Falls
Location: Pisgah National Forest
Directions: FS 477 off US 276; Avery Creek and Buckhorn Gap trails
Description: energetic cascade/plunges
Trail: Moderate; 2 miles
Swimming?: No

Wintergreen Falls (page 18)
Location: DuPont State Forest
Directions: Guion Farms Parking Area off Sky Valley Road Road
Description: 20-foot cascade/plunge over wide rock
Trail: Moderate; 2 miles
Swimming?: Yes, in small plunge pool

Retrieving at French Broad Falls.

Asheville Area Parks By Location

*"I can't think of anything that brings me closer to tears than
when my old dog - completely exhausted after a hard day
in the field - limps away from her nice spot in front of the fire
and comes over to where I'm sitting and puts her head in my lap,
a paw over my knee, and closes her eyes, and goes back to sleep.
I don't know what I've done to deserve that kind of friend."*
-Gene Hill

Other Books On Hiking With Your Dog from Cruden Bay Books
www.hikewithyourdog.com

DOGGIN' AMERICA: 100 Ideas For Great Vacations To Take With Your Dog - $19.95

DOGGIN' THE MID-ATLANTIC: 400 Tail-Friendly Parks To Hike With Your Dog In New Jersey, Pennsylvania, Delaware, Maryland and Northern Virginia - $18.95

DOGGIN' CLEVELAND: The 50 Best Places To Hike With Your Dog In Northeast Ohio - $12.95

DOGGIN' PITTSBURGH: The 50 Best Places To Hike With Your Dog In Southeast Pennsylvania - $12.95

DOGGIN' ORLANDO: The 30 Best Places To Hike With Your Dog in Central Florida - $9.95

DOGGIN' NORTHWEST FLORIDA: The 50 Best Places To Hike With Your Dog In The Panhandle - $12.95

DOGGIN' ATLANTA: The 50 Best Places To Hike With Your Dog in North Georgia - $12.95

DOGGIN' THE POCONOS: The 33 Best Places To Hike With Your Dog In Pennsylvania's Northeast Mountains - $9.95

DOGGIN' THE BERKSHIRES: The 33 Best Places To Hike With Your Dog In Western Massachusetts - $9.95

DOGGIN' NORTHERN VIRGINIA: The 50 Best Places To Hike With Your Dog In NOVA - $9.95

DOGGIN' DELAWARE: The 40 Best Places To Hike With Your Dog In The First State - $9.95

DOGGIN' MARYLAND: The 100 Best Places To Hike With Your Dog In The Free State - $12.95

DOGGIN' JERSEY: The 100 Best Places To Hike With Your Dog In The Garden State - $12.95

DOGGIN' RHODE ISLAND: The 25 Best Places To Hike With Your Dog In The Ocean State - $7.95

DOGGIN' MASSACHUSETTS: The 100 Best Places To Hike With Your Dog in the Bay State - $12.95

DOGGIN' CONNECTICUT: The 57 Best Places To Hike With Your Dog In The Nutmeg State - $12.95

DOGGIN' THE FINGER LAKES: The 50 Best Places To Hike With Your Dog - $12.95

DOGGIN' LONG ISLAND: The 30 Best Places To Hike With Your Dog In New York's Playground - $9.95

DOGGIN' THE TIDEWATER: The 33 Best Places To Hike With Your Dog from the Northern Neck to Virginia Beach - $9.95

DOGGIN' THE CAROLINA COASTS: The 50 Best Places To Hike With Your Dog Along The North Carolina And South Carolina Shores - $11.95

DOGGIN' AMERICA'S BEACHES: A Traveler's Guide To Dog-Friendly Beaches - $12.95

THE CANINE HIKER'S BIBLE - $19.95

A Bark In The Park: The 55 Best Places To Hike With Your Dog In The Philadelphia Region - $12.95

A Bark In The Park: The 50 Best Places To Hike With Your Dog In The Baltimore Region - $12.95

A Bark In The Park: The 37 Best Places To Hike With Your Dog In Pennsylvania Dutch Country - $9.95

Made in the USA
Lexington, KY
22 October 2012